Key Issues in Early Years Education

Key Issues in Early Years Education is the second edition of *The Early Years: a reader*. This essential text for students and professionals is unique in its range of voices and topics and in its determination to see the child as central to learning and development. As in the first edition it not only has chapters written by key figures in the field of early childhood education and care but also by students on a range of early childhood programmes. Notable key figures from the first edition have been added to to include Helen Penn, Henrietta Dombey, Hilary Faust and Charmian Kenner. Rosemary Nalden, who is involved in significant work with children in South Africa, has added her voice to give us examples of children acting both as learners and teachers.

This fully revised collection is a comprehensive investigation into the key issues in early years education which:

- provides a blend of real life examples and theory, drawn from a diversity of early childhood settings and classes;
- is written in an accessible voice;
- brings theory to life by linking it with practice;
- examines how children explore, express and represent their worlds.

Many of the original sections have been revised and updated to take account of changes to the education system over the last decade. Two new sections in this edition are (a) *Children as thinkers and problem-solvers* and (b) *Learning: a second chance*, which looks at adults learning something new and considers the similarities and differences that might exist between them and children.

This fascinating and highly readable book will be of interest to teachers, practitioners, students and anyone concerned with the care and education of our youngest children.

Sandra Smidt is a writer and consultant in early years.

Key Issues in Early Years Education

A guide for students and practitioners

Second edition

Edited by Sandra Smidt

 Routledge
Taylor & Francis Group

LONDON AND NEW YORK

First edition published 1998, as *The Early Years: A Reader*,
by Routledge
Second edition published 2010
by Routledge
2 Park Square, Milton Park, Abingdon, Oxon OX14 4RN

Simultaneously published in the USA and Canada
by Routledge
270 Madison Avenue, New York, NY 10016

*Routledge is an imprint of the Taylor & Francis Group,
an informa business*

Typeset in Bembo by Swales & Willis Ltd, Exeter, Devon
Printed and bound in Great Britain by
TJ International, Padstow, Cornwall

British Library Cataloguing in Publication Data
A catalogue record for this book is available from the British
Library

Library of Congress Cataloging-in-Publication Data
Key issues in early years education : a guide for students and
practitioners / Sandra Smidt.
    p. cm.
    Rev. ed. of: The early years, c2010.
    1. Early childhood education. 2. Child development.
    3. Education, Preschool. 4. Play. I. Smidt, Sandra, 1943-
    II. Smidt, Sandra, 1943- Early years.
    LB1139.23.E276 2010
    372.210941—dc22   2009003843

ISBN13: 978–0–415–46526–7 (hbk)
ISBN13: 978–0–415–46525–0 (pbk)

ISBN10: 0–415–46526–5 (hbk)
ISBN10: 0–415–46525–7 (pbk)

The material in this reader was originally published by the
University of North London Press in the course reader for the
Early Childhood Studies Scheme: *I seed it and feeled it: Young
Children Learning* (1996). The editor and publisher are grateful for
the university's kind permission to reproduce it here.

To honour the memory of Gift

Contents

Preface
A short history of this book

This book arose out of the development of the Early Childhood Studies Scheme as a distance learning programme during the mid-1990s, at what was the University of North London. The intention was to produce a book which would, in effect, be a course reader for students learning either independently at home or following taught programmes and the book was made up of chapters written by key figures in the field of early childhood education and care and by students studying on the Early Childhood Studies Scheme. This made the book unique in terms of its range of voices, attention to issues beyond just school or nursery and determination to see the child as central to learning and development.

The first edition was published in-house by the university and was entitled '*I seed it and feeled it*': *Young Children Learning* (1996). The title was chosen to indicate that the book was concerned with how children, encountering something new, use all their senses in order to make sense of what they have encountered and in doing this reveal something of the processes we call 'learning'. In 1998, Routledge agreed to publish the book but regarded the title as too 'vague' and opted, instead, for *The Early Years: A Reader*. That was ten years ago and the book has remained of interest to many of those involved in the care, education and development of young learners, despite many changes in terms of government policy, climate and values and a growing culture of testing, measuring and rating children and their settings. In 2007 Routledge proposed a new edition of the book and a new title – this time, *Key Issues in Early Years Education*. It is for you, the reader, to judge which of the book's three titles speaks most directly to you.

Those of you reading this book who have read the first edition will find much that is familiar. Some of the pieces written by key figures have been updated: others remain as they were. Some of the work of students has been retained, although it has been almost impossible to contact those students, so we do hope those whose work is retained are happy with it and we apologise to those whose work could not be kept in this edition. Very few pieces of work from students currently following programmes at a range of universities have been found and included. Some of the parts of the book have been cut because we feel it important to bring the key sections up-to-date and add additional pieces to them, which means that less well-argued sections have had to go. We remain determined that: (a) the child remains central to the process and (b) learning and development are seen as holistic. You will find little or no mention of standards or levels or targets but much, we hope, which reminds you of how hard children work to make sense of the world. You will also find much to help you appreciate what it is that good educators and early years workers do and just how much they need to know about learning, development and culture to do this sensitively and respectfully.

What the new edition looks like

Introduction. The book opens with a review of changes since the first edition. This is followed by a key chapter written by Lilian Katz, which will be familiar to those of you who knew the first edition.

Part I: How young children learn remains, but has been added to. It has become, per-haps, the most important part of this book. We all felt there was a serious omission from the original section in terms of not having a focus on childhoods other than Western and privileged ones. The original chapter by Lilian Katz has been retained but we also invited Helen Penn to add her strong, important and thoughtful views. Janet Moyles has updated her chapter which is still about play and which argues, powerfully, that we still have a long way to go in this country to understand what play is and why it matters.

Part II: Understanding children remains, because we still regard observation as a key tool of any early childhood worker, as can be seen from the chapter by Gillian Allery. The seminal chapter by Mary Jane Drummond has been updated and is supported by some of the sensitive and perceptive observations of children from the first edition. In this part too, we think about schemas and Fran Paffard has updated her chapter in light of both her experience and her reading.

Part III: All our children is retained and strengthened. A key chapter by Birgit Voss has been updated and we have commissioned a new chapter from Charmian Kenner. In this chapter she helps us understand how children with more than language can both teach and learn from one another. Also in this part is a piece of work written by a current student, Jacintha Moore.

Part IV: Children as thinkers and problem-solvers is a new section, which looks at how children, through their investigations and experience, begin to ask and answer their own questions and develop their own ideas and sometimes theories. The key chap-ter in this section has been written by Hilary Faust who looks at ways of helping chil-dren to think mathematically. Also included is some of the work of students from the first edition, which illustrate children posing and answering questions.

Part V: Understanding the written world starts with a key chapter by Henrietta Dombey who offers a very reasoned critique of some current trends in teaching and learning, together with timely reminders of how to create literacy-rich learning environments to tempt children into being readers and writers. Gillian Lathey has updated her original chapter and Evelyn Slavid, who wrote about how her daughter Jessica learned to read, has asked Jess herself to reflect on the role of books and reading in her life. Sandra Smidt wrote about her first grandchild, Hannah, and the role books and stories played in her life when she was a baby and toddler. Hannah is now 13 years old and still an avid and critical reader.

Part VI: Representing thoughts and feelings. Emma Stoddart and Duane Hernandez give valuable contributions to this section. The key chapter in this section actually provides a link between this section and the final section. It is a chapter written by Rosemary Nalden who became well known for the remarkable work she does via classical music with young black children in South Africa. This is supported by some of the student work from the previous edition.

Part VII: Learning: A second chance. This section looks at adults learning a new skill late in life and examines where this is similar to or different from the learning of young children. The key voices in this part are those of adults who have started to learn something new later in life and who talk of 'Late early learning'. In this part, you will read the work of Gillian Gould, Sandra Smidt, Richard Gartner and Jenny Thornley.

Introduction

During the almost 12 years since the first edition of this book there have been enormous changes in this country politically, economically, socially and educationally. In terms of the changes for children, perhaps most dramatic has been the determination to measure them and their learning and development with an assumption that measuring or testing children will make them, in some way, better or better at whatever it is that is being measured. For example, we now have cohorts of children who have been defined as being gifted and talented at maths or literacy or physical education or art. The impact of this culture of testing on children has been dramatic and very often negative. Children assume that they will have tests on a regular basis and that their schools will be rated according to how well they and their peers perform on a particular day on a range of decontextualised tasks. For the youngest children, this culture of testing has led them to believe, very early on, that there are some things that they cannot do. A culture of failure has developed along with a culture which deprives children of independence and encourages them to be wary of others, to be reluctant to take risks and to spend a great deal of time watching screens of one type or another. There is a growing awareness that some things need to change so that childhood can be enjoyed rather than endured. But many feel there is still a long way to go before young children can be curious and investigative and able to express their thoughts and ideas, ask their questions, test their hypotheses, paint their dreams, and explore the world without continually being watched and tested.

In terms of early childhood education, much has changed. In 1996 the early childhood studies scheme at the then University of North London was the first of its kind in the country. It had been developed precisely to allow those from non-traditional educational backgrounds to gain access to Higher Education and to work, full or part-time, and later to study, by face-to-face or by distance learning, towards an accredited and recognised qualification. Other universities followed this lead and now early childhood or childhood degrees proliferate and those working with young children have become experts in the field, knowing a great deal about complex things, such as learning and development, the effects of poverty, nutrition and health, the importance of respecting diversity, and so on. In many schools and settings you will now find people who have completed such degrees, often taking a long time to do so because of having to work in order to support families as they study. Their voices can be found in this book. In our schools and settings we find childcare workers, nursery nurses, teaching assistants, teachers, coordinators, bilingual workers – a range of people from a range of backgrounds offering children different role models and styles of interaction and support. This is, of course, very positive and something to be celebrated.

Alongside this is the increased visibility of early childhood issues and perhaps a growing awareness of where this country sits relative to others in both the developed and the developing worlds. Twelve years ago parents could, theoretically, choose to have their youngest children at home with them, or send them to a playgroup or employ a childminder or a nanny. Childminders were sometimes regulated and premises approved. The children regarded as being most at risk were sometimes and in some places offered a free place in a nursery centre, run by social services and sometimes employing people trained to work with young children. The most fortunate could send their children to a nursery school where all the staff had some relevant training in aspects of learning, but perhaps little in terms of aspects of care. The places were free but few and often confined to larger cities. Some schools had nursery classes, with trained staff, but under the direction of a headteacher who might or might not have had specific training about the needs of young children. Many children spent half-days in playgroups, often run by parents and in inappropriate facilities. So it was a very mixed bag and the issue of choice was choice by affordability, postcode and luck. At the same time, children in Reggio Emilia in Italy were enjoying the fantastic facilities on offer at the *asili nidi* (the facilities for babies and toddlers) and the *scuole materne* (the first formal learning facilities) that have now become so famous.

When the labour government was elected in the late 1990s, there was a sense that offering more in the way of childcare and provision for children before starting school would be a priority. Margaret Hodge, as leader of Islington council prior to that election, had made 'Under Fives' a priority and started what became something of a trend. A number of advisory documents were produced and the massive SureStart project launched. A curriculum for children from three to nearly six was produced – the Foundation Stage curriculum, and a welcome, if not universal, move was made to ensure that all children in all settings had access to outdoor play at all times. Then, in 2006 the new Childcare Act was announced together with a 10-year childcare strategy 'Choice for parents, the best start for children'. This set the context for the Early Years Foundation Stage, the new and statutory curriculum which builds on and replaces the Curriculum Guidance for the Foundation Stage, Birth to Three Matters and the National Standards for Under 8s Day-care and Childminding. In September 2008 it became mandatory for all schools and early years' providers in settings which are registered by OFSTED to adhere to this curriculum for all children from birth to the end of the academic year in which a child has his or her fifth birthday.

There is no space here to go into any of this in detail. Many are deeply concerned that this should be statutory; others are concerned that it refers to early learning goals, which include things like expecting children at the end of the stage to 'hear and say sounds in words in the order in which they occur' or 'link sounds to letters, naming and sounding the letters of the alphabet'. Yet, there is some reassurance in the fact that this Early Years Foundation Stage (EYFS) focuses on the child, inviting practitioners to watch children and listen to them and use this as the basis for planning.

This is a book about children and written for those who work with them to help them develop and learn from all their experiences and through all their interactions. It is a book which celebrates children's curiosity, individuality, eagerness to know and ability to question. It is a book which also celebrates the efforts of those who work with these children and enjoy their questions, their answers, their offerings and their individuality.

The first piece in the book is the same as the first piece in the previous edition. It is a contextualising piece written by Lilian Katz, who is famous throughout much of the world for her work in the field of early childhood and for her views on being respectful of children and their thinking. Katz addresses philosophical and theoretical rather than practice issues and in the first chapter, she offers ideas which may be new and sometimes difficult to absorb, but the closing line of the piece is something worth reading over and over: '… to care for and about others' children is not just practical; it is also right'.

Chapter 1

What is basic for young children?

Lilian G. Katz

Lilian G. Katz is Professor Emerita of Elementary and Early Childhood Education at the University of Illinois (Urbana-Champaign) and is currently Co-Director of the Clearinghouse on Early Education and Parenting (CEEP) at the University of Illinois. Professor Katz is the author of more than 100 publications, including articles, chapters and books about early childhood education, teacher education, child development and parenting of young children. She and her late husband Boris Katz have three grown children, five grandsons and one grand-daughter.

A group of young college students were discussing their reactions to their teaching practice experiences. One described her experience in deeply disappointed tones. Among her complaints was that the programme director refused to let the children have small animals in the nursery. I listened appreciatively for a while to the righteous indignation only the young and inexperienced can enjoy. I then asked her as gently as I could: 'What are the chances that a child can develop into a competent adult without having had animals to play with in the nursery?' 'In other words', I said 'what do you believe is really basic for young children?' A lively discussion followed, leading all of us to search our own assumptions for answers to the question: What does each child have to have for optimum development? My answer to this question is outlined below by offering six interrelated propositions that I hope will be helpful to you as you inspect your own answers to the same question.

All six propositions below rest on the assumption that whatever is good for children is only good for them in the 'right' proportions. In other words, just because something is good for children, more of it is not necessarily better for them. This generalisation applies to so many influences on children's development that I refer to it as the 'principle of optimum effects'. Among the many examples are attention, affection, stimulation, independence, novelty, choices of activities and so on. All of these can be thought to be good for children, but only in optimum amounts, frequencies or intensities. Furthermore, what might be optimal for one child might not be for another; that is why it is so important to get to know each child, as well as to know about them. With this principle as backdrop, here is my list of what every child has to have for healthy development.

A sense of safety

The young child has to have a deep sense of safety. I am referring here to psychological safety, which we usually speak of in terms of feeling secure, that is the subjective feeling of being strongly connected and deeply attached to one or more others. Experiencing oneself as attached, connected – safe – comes not just from being loved, but from feeling loved, feeling wanted, feeling significant, to an optimum (not maximum) degree. Note that the emphasis is more on feeling loved and wanted than on being loved and wanted. There are, no doubt, many children who are loved, but for a wide variety of reasons, do not necessarily feel loved.

As I understand early development, feeling strongly attached comes not just from the warmth and kindness of parents and caregivers. The feelings are a consequence of children perceiving that what they do or do not do really matters to others – matters so much that others will pick them up, comfort them, get angry and even scold them. Safety, then, grows out of being able to trust people to respond not just warmly but authentically, intensely and honestly.

Optimum self-esteem

This proposition applies to all children, whether they live in wealthy or poor environments, whether they are at home or at school, whether they have special needs or typical needs, whatever their age, gender, race, ethnic group or nationality. Every child has to have optimal – not excessive – self-esteem.

One does not acquire self-esteem at a certain moment in childhood and then have it forever. Self-esteem is nurtured by and responsive to significant others: adults, siblings and other children, throughout the growing years. Even more important to keep in mind here is that one cannot have self-esteem in a vacuum. Self-esteem is the effect of our evaluations of ourselves against criteria that we acquire very early in life. We acquire these criteria from our families, neighbourhoods, cultures, ethnic groups and later on from peer groups and the larger community. These criteria against which we come to evaluate ourselves as acceptable and worthwhile, and against which we evaluate and experience ourselves as lovable may vary from family to family. In some families, beauty is an important criterion for esteem; in others, neatness or athletic ability or toughness are the criteria against which one's worth is evaluated or estimated. Consider for a moment that such personal attributes as being dainty, quiet, garrulous, pious, well-mannered or academically precocious, might constitute the criteria against which the young children we serve are evaluated as being estimable.

It is, of course, the right, if not the duty, of each family to establish what it considers to be the criteria against which each member is judged acceptable and upon which esteem is based. The processes and the patterns by which these judgements are implemented are not likely to occur at a conscious level in either formulation or expression.

One of our responsibilities as educators is to be sensitive to the criteria of self-esteem that children bring with them to the early childhood setting. We may not agree with the family's definition of the 'good boy' or the 'good girl', but we would be very unwise to downgrade, undermine, or in other ways violate the self-esteem criteria that children bring with them to the early childhood setting. At the same time, we must also help children acquire criteria in the setting that serves to protect the welfare of the whole group of children for whom we are responsible. I cannot think of any way in which it could be helpful to children to undermine their respect for their own families.

Feeling that life is worth living

Every child has to feel that life is worth living, reasonably satisfying and interesting most of the time, and authentic. This proposition suggests that we involve children in activities and interactions about activities which are real and significant to them, and which are intriguing and absorbing to them. I have in mind here the potential hazard inherent in modern industrialised societies of creating environments and experiences for young children which are superficial, phony, frivolous and trivial. I suggest also that we resist the temptation to settle for activities that merely amuse and titillate children. Thus, criteria for selecting activities might include that they (a) give children opportunities to examine their own experiences and to reconstruct their own environments and that they (b) give adults opportunities to help children learn what meanings to assign to their own experiences.

Visits to early childhood programmes around the world often provoke me to wonder whether we have taken our longstanding emphasis on warmth and kindness, acceptance and love to mean simply 'Let's be nice to children'. As I watch adults being nice and kind and gentle, I wonder also whether if I were a child in such pleasant environments I would look at the adults and ask myself something like 'Everybody is kind and sweet, but inside them is there anybody home?'

Children should be able to experience their lives throughout their growing years as real and satisfying, whether they are at home, in childcare centres, in playgroups, or in schools.

Help with making sense of experience

Young children need adults and others who help them make sense of their own experiences. By the time we meet the young children in our care, they have already constructed some understandings of their experiences. Many of their understandings or constructions are likely to be inaccurate or incorrect, though developmentally appropriate. As I see it, our major responsibility is to help the young to improve, extend, refine, develop and deepen their own understandings or constructions of their own worlds. As they grow older and reach primary school age, it is our responsibility to help them develop understandings of other people's experiences, people who are distant in both time and place. Indeed, increasing refinement and deepening of understandings is, ideally, a lifelong process.

We might ask: 'What do young children need or want to make sense of?' Certainly of people, of what they do, and why they do it, of what and how they feel; and of themselves and other living things around them, how they themselves and other living things grow; where people and things come from, and how things are made and how they work, and so forth.

If we are to help young children improve and develop their understandings of their experiences, we must uncover what those understandings are. The uncovering that we do, and that occurs as children engage in the activities we provide, helps us to make good decisions about what to 'cover' next and what follow-up activities to plan. Keep in mind that one of our responsibilities as teachers is to educate children's interests.

Authoritative adults

Young children have to be around adults who accept the authority that is theirs by virtue of their greater experience, knowledge and wisdom. This proposition is based on the assumption that neither parents nor educators are caught between the extremes of authoritarianism or permissiveness (Baumrind 1971). Authoritarianism may be defined as the exercise of power without warmth, encouragement or explanation. Permissiveness may be seen as the abdication of adult authority and power, although it may offer children warmth, encouragement and support as they seem to need it. I am suggesting that instead of the extremes of authoritarianism and permissiveness, young children have to have around them adults who are authoritative – adults who exercise their very considerable power over the lives of young children with warmth, support, encouragement and adequate explanations of the limits they impose upon them. The concept of authoritativeness also includes treating children with respect – treating their opinions, feelings, wishes and ideas as valid even when we disagree with them. To respect people we agree with is not a great problem; respecting those whose ideas, wishes and feelings are different from ours or troubling to us, may be a mark of wisdom in parents and of genuine professionalism in teachers and childcare workers.

Desirable role models

Young children need optimum association with adults and older children who exemplify the personal qualities we want them to acquire. Make your own list of the qualities you want the young children for whom you are responsible to acquire. There may be some differences among us, but it is very likely that there are some qualities we can agree that we want all children to have: the capacity to care for and about others, the disposition to be honest, kind, accepting of those who are different from ourselves, to love learning, and so forth.

This proposition suggests that we inspect children's environments and ask: To what extent do our children have contact with people who exhibit these qualities?' To what extent do our children observe people who are counter-examples of the qualities we want to foster, but who are also presented as glamorous and attractive?' It seems to me that children need neighbourhoods and communities (as well as the media) which take the steps necessary to protect them from excessive exposure to violence and crime during the early years while their characters are still in formation.

Children need relationships and experience with adults who are willing to take a stand on what is worth doing, worth having, worth knowing and worth caring about. This proposition seems to belabour the obvious. But in an age of increasing emphasis on pluralism, multiculturalism and community participation, professionals are increasingly hesitant and apologetic about their own values. It seems to me that such hesitancy to take a stand on what is worthwhile may cause us to give children unclear signals about what is worth knowing and doing and what is expected.

Taking a stand on what we value does not guarantee that our children will accept or agree with us. Nor does it imply that we reject others' versions of the 'good life'. We must, in fact, cultivate our capacities to respect alternative definitions of the 'good life'. My point is that when we take a stand, with quiet conviction and courage, we help the young to see us as thinking and caring individuals who have enough self-respect to act on our own values and to give clear signals about what those values are.

In summary, these six propositions are related to our responsibilities for the quality of the daily lives of all our children – wherever they spend those days, throughout the years of growth and development. We must come to see that the wellbeing of our children, of each and every child, is intimately and inextricably linked to the wellbeing of all children. When one of our own children needs lifesaving surgery, someone else's child will perform it. When one of our own children is struck down by violence, someone else's child will have inflicted it. The wellbeing of our own children can be secured only when the wellbeing of other people's children is also secure. But to care for and about others' children is not just practical; it is also right.

Reference

Baumrind, D. (1971) 'Current patterns of parental authority', *Developmental Psychology Monographs* 4: 1–102.

Part I

How young children learn

Much has been written about how young children learn. Piaget believed that young children learn through two processes which he called assimilation and accommodation. He saw young children not as empty vessels waiting to be filled up with knowledge, but actively seeking to understand the world in which they live. Through exploring their world using their movements and their senses, they begin to find patterns which allow them to categorise and classify things. Piaget believed that the role of adults in supporting learning was to provide children with a rich and stimulating environment, full of things they could explore. For him the interaction between child and adult was not essential. Vygotsky and Bruner, by contrast, believed that talk and interaction were essential for learning. For them, the role of the adult was more complex and learning more social than for Piaget. Over the past 12 years, we might argue that there have been two competing strands of development. One is a recognition of the importance of adopting a sociocultural and sociohistorical view of learning and development which sees the child as coming with a unique history and culture, which is his or her foundation for learning. The other is seeing the child as a potential consumer and educating the child to fulfil this role.

Nothing, however, disproves the evidence of how complex early learning is. The work of researchers, such as Colwyn Trevarthen (1988) has demonstrated that the connections between brain cells are laid down most rapidly in the early years and that the development of these connections – the very essence of learning and thinking – depends on stimulation. In some sectors of society, this has been misinterpreted to imply that learning requires expensive and specially produced equipment. Margaret Donaldson (1978) has shown how hard children work to bring their previous experience to bear on new situations and how important it is for children to consolidate their new learning in situations which allow this. Donaldson and others have shown how young children, exposed at too early an age to formal decontextualised learning, learn failure. Donaldson argues powerfully that young children, in order to be able to build on what they already know and can do, need to be in situations which make 'human sense' to them.

There are three key chapters in this part and it opens with one arguing the importance of play as a mode of learning and written by Lilian Katz. You may remember it from the first edition. Since the first edition, some people have started to question whether this emphasis on 'play' is very 'Western' and so, to redress the balance, we have invited Helen Penn to add her views. There is then an updated chapter on play by Janet Moyles.

Chapter 2

A developmental approach to the curriculum in the early years

Lilian G. Katz

In this chapter, Lilian argues that what is learned, and how it is best learned, depends on the age of the child. She goes on to say that how something is learned depends on what the something is as well as on the particular developmental characteristics of the learner. In essence, she poses three questions:

1 What do we think young children should be learning?
2 When should they be learning it?
3 How will it best be learned?

These questions are pivotal and are themes which are addressed throughout many of the pieces in this book.

Everyone responsible for planning a curriculum must address the following three questions:

1 What should be learned?
2 When should it be learned?
3 How is it best learned?

Responses to the first question provide the goals of the programme for which peda-gogical practices are to be adopted. The second question is developmental, in that it draws upon what is known about the development of the learner. In other words, child development helps to address the questions of programme design. The third question turns specifically to matters of appropriate pedagogy itself; it includes con-sideration of all aspects of implementing a programme by which the programme's goals can be achieved, depending on what is to be learned, and when it is to be learned. In other words, responses to one of the three questions are inextricably linked to responses to the other two.

Thus, what should be learned and how it is best learned depends on when the learning is to occur. Similarly, how something is learned depends upon what it is, as well as upon the developmental characteristics of the learner. For example, virtually all stakeholders in early childhood education would place literacy high on the list of answers to the question, 'What should be learned?' However, they are likely to diverge considerably upon the question of when as well as how it should be learned – the latter considerations being related to each other. Terms such as emergent literacy and pre-literacy have recently appeared in the early childhood literature, partly in order to address the confounding of the when and how questions. Even although the three questions are clearly linked, for the sake of discussion, they are taken up separately below.

What should be learned?

The values and preferences of the parents served by the programme would seem to have first claim among criteria for determining what should be learned. However, parents are rarely a homogeneous or monolithic group with a clear consensus about the goals of their children's education. While the community and parents' preferences contribute to determining the goals, the special expertise of professional educators should be brought to bear on addressing the questions of when and how the goals can be best implemented.

Four types of learning goals

Whatever specific learning goals and objectives are identified by clients and educators, they are all likely to fit into each of four types of learning goals:

1   Knowledge/understanding
2   Skills
3   Dispositions
4   Feelings.

These can be defined as follows:

Knowledge/understanding

During the preschool period, this can be broadly defined as ideas, concepts, constructions, schemas, facts, information, stories, customs, myths, songs and other such contents of mind that come under the heading of what is to be learned. Three Piagetian categories of knowledge – social, physical and logico–mathematical – are often used in discussions of the knowledge goals in early childhood education. The term understanding is appended here to bring attention to the importance of understanding ideas rather than just simply knowing the words or names of things, e.g. knowing the days of the week does not necessarily mean that a child understands fully its implications.

Skills

These are defined as small, discrete and relatively brief units of behaviour that are easily observed or inferred from behaviour (e.g. skills such as cutting, drawing, counting a group of objects, adding, subtracting, friendship-making, problem-solving skills, and so on).

Dispositions

These are broadly defined as relatively enduring 'habits of mind', or characteristic ways of responding to experience across types of situations (including persistence at a task, curiosity, generosity, meanness, the disposition to read, to solve problems). Unlike an item of knowledge or a skill, a disposition is not an end-state to be mastered once and for all. It is a trend or consistent pattern of behaviour and its possession is established only if its manifestation is observed repeatedly. Thus a person's disposition to be a reader, for example, can only be ascertained if he or she is observed to read spontaneously, frequently and without external coercion.

Feelings

These are subjective emotional or affective states, e.g. feelings of belonging, of self-esteem, confidence, adequacy and inadequacy, feelings of competence and incompetence, and so forth. Feelings about or towards significant phenomena may range from being transitory or enduring, intense or weak, or perhaps ambivalent. In early childhood education, attitudes and values can also be included in this category; in education for older children they merit separate categories.[1]

In principle, pedagogical practices are developmentally and educationally appropriate if they address all four categories of learning goals equally and simultaneously. Pedagogical practices are not appropriate if they emphasise the acquisition of knowledge and the mastery of skills without ensuring developmentally reasonable understanding, and that the dispositions to use the knowledge and skills so learned are also strengthened. Similarly, if the desired knowledge and skills are mastered in such a way that dislike of them or their use or of the school environment itself develops throughout the learning process; in such cases the pedagogy may be judged inappropriate. Similarly, if a pedagogical approach succeeds in generating feelings of joy, pleasure, amusement, or excitement, but fails to bring about the acquisition of desirable knowledge, understanding and skills, it cannot be judged appropriate.

Most stakeholders in early childhood education are likely to agree on broad goals in all four categories of learning. For example, most education authorities' curriculum guides list such goals as knowledge and skills related to literacy and numeracy and various items of cultural knowledge, plus such dispositions as the desire to learn, creativity, cooperativeness, and so forth; the list of goals related to feelings usually includes 'positive feelings about themselves', or 'self-confidence'.[2]

Once the knowledge, skills, dispositions and feelings to be learned have been agreed upon, the next question is when they should be learned.

When should it be learned?

Learning in the four types of learning goals proposed above occurs constantly, whether intentionally or incidentally. However, a developmental approach to curriculum planning takes into account both of the two dimensions of development: the normative and the dynamic dimensions. These two equally important dimensions of development are defined as follows.

Normative dimensions

The *normative dimension* of development addresses the characteristics and capabilities of children that are typical or 'normal' for their age group (e.g. the typical size of vocabulary of 4–year-olds, the average age of first walking or of understanding numerical concepts).

Age norms also provide useful starting points for curriculum planning. Knowledge of age-typical interests, activities and abilities can provide a basis for preliminary planning of a general programme of activities, and the selection of equipment and materials. For example, norms of development provide a basis for assuming that most 2-year-olds need daytime naps, most 4-year-olds do not understand calendar concepts fully, or that, typically, most 5-year-olds can begin to write their own names, etc.

Age norms are also useful for alerting teachers to individual children whose patterns of development depart noticeably from those of their age group and who warrant close observation by which to ascertain whether special curriculum and teaching strategies are required.

Dynamic dimensions

The *dynamic dimension* of development deals with an individual child's progress from immaturity to maturity. This dimension addresses changes over time within an individual and the long-term effects of early experience rather than the normality or typicality of behaviour and abilities of an age group. This dimension has three aspects:

1   Sequence, refers to the order or stages of development through which an individual passes, e.g. in achieving mastery of first language. The curriculum and teaching practices consider what learning and developmental tasks have to be completed before the next learning can occur. For example, it is reasonable to assume that introduction to a second language is most likely to be beneficial following mastery of one's first language.

2   Delayed effects refer to the potential positive and negative effects of early experience that are not manifested at the time of occurrence, but may influence

later functioning (e.g. early infant–caregiver attachment may influence later parenting competence). Some practices that are effective in the short term may have delayed or 'sleeper' effects that are deleterious in the long term (e.g. rewards and punishments, unsatisfactory early bonding and attachment, etc.). Some practices that may not seem important to development during the early years may have positive delayed effects later. Whether positive or negative, 'delayed effects' are those that do not show up until later in the course of development.

3   Cumulative effects refer to experiences that may have no effects (either positive or negative) if they are occasional or rare, but may have powerful effects if frequent (e.g. the cumulative positive effects of frequent block play or cumulative negative effects of frequent even though mild criticism).

A developmental approach to curriculum and teaching practices takes into account both dimensions of development in that what young children should do and should learn is determined on the basis of what is thought to be best for their development in the long term (i.e. the dynamic consequences of early experience) rather than simply what works in the short term.

How is it best learned?

This question takes us directly to matters of pedagogy, such as consideration of teaching methods, activities, materials and all other practical matters designed to achieve the learning goals, and to take into account what is known about learners' development.

Learning in the four categories of goals is facilitated in different ways. In the case of both *knowledge/understanding and skills*, learning can be aided by instruction as well as by other processes. However, *dispositions and feelings* cannot be learned from direct instruction. Many important dispositions are inborn – e.g. the disposition to learn, to observe, to investigate, to be curious, etc. Many dispositions appear to be learned from models, are strengthened by being manifested and appreciated, and are weakened when unacknowledged or ineffective.

Feelings related to school experiences are learned as by-products of experiences rather than from instruction. Both dispositions and feelings can be thought of as incidental learning in that they are incidental to the processes by which knowledge/understanding and skills are acquired. To label feelings as incidental is not to belittle them, or to devalue the role of pedagogy in their development; rather, it is to emphasise that they cannot be taught didactically. Children cannot be instructed in what feelings to have.

Recent insights into children's development suggest that in principle, the younger the child, the more readily knowledge is acquired through active and interactive processes; conversely, with increasing age, children become more able to profit from reactive, passive–receptive pedagogical approaches or instructional processes. In other words, pedagogical practices are developmentally appropriate when the knowledge to be acquired or constructed is related to the child's own first-hand, direct experiences and when it is accessible from primary sources. This is not to say that children do not acquire knowledge and information from such secondary sources as stories, books and films. The extent to which they do so is related to whether young children can connect the materials within the secondary sources to the images and knowledge they already possess. With increasing age and experience, children become more able to profit from second-hand, indirect experiences and secondary sources.

Thus pedagogical practices are appropriate if they provide young children with ample opportunity to interact with adults and children who are like and unlike themselves, with materials, and directly with real objects and real environments. However, interactions cannot occur in a vacuum; they have to have content. Interactions must be about something – ideally something that interests and matters to the interactors.

What criteria can be used to determine what knowledge or content is appropriate for young children? For example, should young children spend up to 10 or 15 minutes per day in a calendar exercise? Should young children in southern Florida be making snowflake crystals out of Styrofoam at Christmas time? Should substantial amounts of time be allocated to observance of public holidays and festivals? Why? And why not? What factors, data or other matters should be taken into account in answering questions such as these?

One way to approach these questions is to derive principles of practice from what is known about the nature of children's intellectual development. In principle, a substantial proportion of the content of interaction should be related to matters of actual or potential interest to the children served by the programme. Since not all of children's interests are equally deserving of attention, some selection of which interests are the most worthy of promotion is required. Current views of children's learning and their active construction of knowledge suggest that those interests most likely to extend, deepen and improve their understanding of their own environments and experiences are most worth strengthening during the early years.

Notes

1 In the case of young children, undesirable attitudes and values are assumed to be a function of faulty developmental progress rather than of general institutional socialisation. For example, dishonesty or greed in a 5-year-old are more likely to be interpreted as symptoms of poor child-rearing or psychosocial environmental influences, rather than as problems of attitudes and values *per se*.

2 See, e.g., State of Iowa, Kindergarten: A Year of Beginnings, Des Moines, Iowa, 1983; State of Connecticut, A Guide to Program Development for Kindergarten, Part 1 (1988) Harford, CT: State Board of Education; Oklahoma State Department of Education, Beginnings: Early Childhood Education in Oklahoma, 3rd edn, Oklahoma City, OK: State Department of Education 1986; Patricia Morgan Roberts, (ed.) Growing Together: Early Childhood Education in Pennsylvania (Harrisburg) PA: Pennsylvania Department of Education, 1989.

Lilian Katz writes powerfully about the importance of children exploring real things rather than trivia and about the significance of others in children's learning. She offers us much to think about and consider. To widen the argument we now turn to a very different piece, this one written by Professor Helen Penn. She is concerned that we cannot continue to consider childhood or learning or parenting in a very Western sense but have to ensure that we understand something about how very different the experiences of children throughout the world are.

Chapter 3

Does it matter what country you are in?

Are all children the same everywhere or does it matter where you are?

Helen Penn

Helen Penn is Professor of Early Childhood at the University of East London. For the last ten years she has specialised in international policy on early childhood. She has worked in many European countries, but has also explored early education and care in the ex-communist countries of Central Asia – Mongolia, Kazakhstan and Kyrgyzstan – as well as in Namibia, South Africa, Swaziland, Tanzania and Zimbabwe. She has acted as a consultant to many international agencies including the EU, OECD and the Asian Development Bank, and for charities such as Save the Children UK and CfBT Educational Trust. Her recent book, *Quality in Early Education and Care – International Perspectives*, discusses the issues raised in this chapter in more detail.

Geography makes a profound difference. The ease or difficulty of everyday life, the terrain where you live, the community in which you are brought up all make an enormous difference to your life chances and to the kind of person you are able to become. We tend to take the middle-class standards of the rich countries of the North (in Europe and North America) as a norm for child development and education. Yet even within one country, the UK, the variation in the circumstances of children is enormous. Consider the difference, for example, in being a Bangladeshi child in Bradford, or from an upper class family with an estate near Oxford. But at least in the UK, these children will both be fed regularly, they will have access to running water and sanitation; they will have a roof over their heads, a nearby school and a local doctor. For most children in the world, around 60 per cent of them, even these basics do not exist.

In our heads we have an image of a successful, competent adult, a robust individual who can exercise constant choice over material resources. We think early education and care should contribute to the way in which children grow up to become such consuming adults. The anthropologist Robert LeVine, describing an American childhood (but it could equally apply to children in most rich countries), puts it like this:

> The American infant has numerous possessions earmarked as belonging to him alone; their number and variety increase as he gets older, permitting him to

experience the boundaries of self represented in his physical environment ... From infancy onwards the child is encouraged to characterize himself in terms of his favourite toys and foods and those he dislikes: his tastes, aversions and consumer preferences are viewed not only as legitimate but as essential aspects of his growing individuality – and a prized quality of an independent person.

(LeVine 2003: 95)

But for most people, adulthood, let alone childhood, offers few opportunities and few choices. In the poorest countries, between 10 and 20 per cent of children never reach the age of five, and the life expectancy rate is below 50 years of age – compared with 79 years in the UK. A majority of children in the world experience chronic poverty, and lack access to clean water and sanitation, decent shelter, adequate nutrition and regular healthcare; many of these children will also lack education. These children experience the world differently – for example they are unlikely to be picky about food, or to have favourite toys or temper tantrums.

The countries of the rich North have agreed, through the United Nations Development Programme, to set Millennium Development Goals (MDG) to try to reduce some of these very gross inequalities between North and South, and in particular to better the position of children. The date for achieving the MDGs is 2015, but on present progress, it is unlikely that a single one of them will be achieved. Unlikely that is, unless we in the North radically reassess our way of life, our patterns of consumption and our ways of relating to and thinking about the environment. Above all, we have to explore and understand the extent of the differences between peoples and communities in the North and South, the privileges we enjoy and how they affect us and how those who are not in a similar privileged position adapt to their precarious circumstances.

These are macro-level issues, the sociopolitical/socioeconomic circumstances which shape how people live their lives, and from which, for most families in poor countries, there is little or no escape. The child psychology which informs early education and care operates at a micro-level; most of the research in the field is carried out in the North, as if these wider socioeconomic circumstances were largely irrelevant, as if the constraints so many children experience are of no consequence, or can be mitigated or overcome by early childhood experiences.

Bruner (2000) argues on the contrary, that 'perhaps even more than with most cultural matters, childrearing practices and beliefs reflect local conceptions of how the world is and how the child should be readied for living it' (Bruner 2000: xi). Bruner's quote comes from the preface of a witty and imaginative book co-edited by an anthropologist and a psychologist, *A World of Babies: Imagined Childcare for Seven Societies* (DeLoache and Gottleib 2000). This offers a series of short childcare manuals of 'best practice' in dealing with babies, as if each manual was written by a leading practitioner from a local community.

Anthropologists have suggested that there are major differences about how young children are taught to relate to one another, how they are taught to speak and learn. Alma Gottleib, an American anthropologist, has questioned the very notion of

attachment, the idea that young children grow and develop through sustaining relationships with one or two caring adults, and describes communities where childcare
is inherently collective, and children show exceptional independence. Gottleib
worked in the Côte d'Ivoire in West Africa, and this is one of the children she
described:

> Chantal, a feisty two year old in our compound disappeared from sight many
> mornings, only to emerge at noon for lunch and then around 5pm for dinner
> preparations. Although she was too young to report on her day's travels, others
> would chronicle them for us; she regularly roved to the farthest ends of this very
> large village and even deep into the forest to join her older siblings and cousins
> working and playing in the fields. With such early independence even toddlers
> are expected to be alert to dangerous wildlife such as snakes and scorpions and
> they should be able to deal with them effectively – including locating and
> wielding a large machete.
>
> (Gottleib 2004: 32)

What Chantal is doing is nearly inconceivable to childhood experts in rich countries,
preoccupied as they are with physical risk and the need for supervising adults and a
protective environment. Despite her lack of language, at 2 years old, Chantal is
secure, autonomous, curious and very capable. She has a sense of direction and a
sense of time. She can use tools effectively. She and her parents are confident that if
there is any kind of hazard she is sufficiently competent to deal with it, by recognising and avoiding it or by calling upon others to help her. I have worked in a pastoral
community in Mongolia where it was normal for children aged 4 or 5 years to be
able to ride a horse across rough terrain for considerable distances, and be capable of
feats of endurance withstanding cold or heat to an unimaginable (to us) degree
(Demberel and Penn 2007). There are many, many other descriptions of childhood,
in particular communities or societies across the world, where the norms and expectations of childhood are intrinsically different from anything we are used to, or
indeed can imagine, in the North.

In one way, children in the South might be regarded as fortunate; often they grow
up in bilingual or multilingual environments. Depending on the language you speak,
you see and hear the world differently. English is a global language, and most native
English speakers see no reason to learn another language. But ways of thinking and
relating to other people is built into language. The terms of deference and familiar-
ity that are applied to different categories of people (older, young, related, not
related, etc.), the idioms and metaphors, what things are called and why they are
called them; the verbs used to describe past, present and future; all these and much
more are encoded in language. And this is before you write the language down, if
indeed it is a written and not a mainly oral language (some of the greatest literature
in the world was not written down but transmitted orally: the Greek writer
Homer, whose stories have lasted for two millennia, never wrote anything down,
but relied on his listeners to tell the stories in their turn). There are still languages

that are mainly oral and depend for their transmission on careful listening skills rather than on writing. If it is a written language, the script may use Roman or Cyrillic letters, or it may be ideographic (based on pictures). It may be read from left to right, right to left, or top to bottom in rows. The reproduction of script may be, as in Arabic, an intensely precise and artistic endeavour. As Mark Abley has explained, language 'articulates a vision of the world, a vision that shapes us as we shape it' (2003: 274) Language determines learning; some ways of learning – for instance learning to listen, to repeat, to recite and to copy – are more useful and appropriate for young children than others, depending on the linguistic circumstances (Street 2005).

The nuclear family itself, which underscores so much of the literature on early childhood, is a recent historical invention not a universal phenomenon. Parenting is not a given. Many societies are profoundly communal, and kinship and community counts for more than individual relationships. Sarah Hrdy (1999), the sociobiologist who has studied mothering across species, especially in humans and the great apes, suggests that from an evolutionary point of view, children had the best chance of survival when they were looked after by groups of women – grandmothers, aunts, cousins, sisters, as well as the mothers themselves. Multiple caretaking was the best protection for children – which goes against the grain of understanding about the nuclear family and the importance of one-to-one relationships. We think it is important to respect individuality; but for others being an individual – on your own and without the constant intimate presence of others – is the worst kind of punishment. The prize-winning Bangladeshi novelist Jhumpa Lahiri (2003) beautifully catches this contrast between the communality of daily life in Bangladesh, and the isolation of daily life in the USA through the eyes of an immigrant woman who is never reconciled to the lack of the presence of her extended family. Another example is offered by the West African film-maker Abderrahmane Sissako whose extraordinary films 'Waiting for Happiness' and 'Bamako' give some idea of this fusion of family and community, of work and leisure. Sissako says of his own childhood that in his family compound there were never less than 35 people. Children may differ from adults in many ways, but do not live separately from them in their own spaces with their own accoutrements.

This chapter offers only the smallest glimpse into the range of experiences and range of possibilities that exist for children. We write and practice what we know best, and most people who write about early education and care, necessarily focus on their own experiences and reflections. I have been fortunate to work in many places in the South, and I am able to speak from a broader experience. But, as sociologists such as Zigmund Bauman (1995) and Luc Boltanski (1999) point out, the world is opening up to us through the media, albeit filtered, and we can no longer ignore it and assume we have a monopoly on knowledge or privilege. We no longer know best. We are increasingly conscious of the wider global picture, and of the global responsibilities which go with our new and painful awareness. In the little world of early childhood, we have many new insights to take on board.

References

Abley, M. (2003) *Spoken Here: Travels Amongst Threatened Languages*, London: Arrow Books.

Bauman, Z. (1995) *Life in Fragments: Essays on Postmodern Morality*, Oxford: Blackwell.

Boltanski, L. (1999) *Distant Suffering: Morality, Media and Politics*, Cambridge: Cambridge University Press.

Bruner, J. (2000). 'Foreword', in J. DeLoache and A. Gottleib (eds) *A World of Babies: Imagined Childcare Guides for Seven Societies*, Cambridge: Cambridge University Press.

DeLoache, J. and Gottleib, A. (eds) (2000) *A World of Babies: Imagined Childcare Guides for Seven Societies*, Cambridge: Cambridge University Press.

Demberel J. and Penn, H. (2007) 'Education and pastoralism in Mongolia', in C. Dyer (ed.) *The Education of Nomadic Principles: Current Issues and Future Prospects*, Oxford: Berghahn Books, p. 193–211.

Gottlieb, A. (2004) *The Afterlife is Where We Come from: The Culture of Infancy in West Africa*, Chicago: University of Chicago Press.

Hrdy, S. (1999) *Mother Nature: Maternal Instincts and How they Shape the Human Species*, New York: Ballantine Books.

Lahiri, J. (2003) *The Namesake*, London: Harper Perennial.

LeVine, R. (2003) *Childhood Socialization: Comparative Studies of Parenting, Learning and Educational Change*, Hong Kong: Comparative Education Research Centre.

Street, B. (ed.) (2005) *Literacies Across Educational Contexts: Mediating Learning and Teaching*. Philadelphia: Caslon.

Penn offers us much to think about and challenges views many of us may have held for years. But her references are familiar. Bruner, for example, is someone we have all certainly heard of and may even have read. She makes us think about some things we pay little attention to – the importance of spoken language, group parenting as opposed to the nuclear family, how children interrogate their world and what is meant by play and independence. Now read what Janet Moyles tells us in the next chapter about play and see how this informs your ideas.

Chapter 4

Play

The powerful means of learning in the early years

Janet Moyles

Janet Moyles is Professor Emeritus, Anglia Ruskin University and a play/early years consultant. She has worked as an early years teacher and head, and has written and edited widely, including *The Excellence of Play* (OUP, 2005) and *Effective Leadership and Management in the Early Years* (OUP, 2007). She has directed several research projects including Jills of All Trades? (ATL, 1996), Too Busy to Play? (Esmee Fairbairn Trust/University of Leicester, 1997–2000), SPEEL (Study of Pedagogical Effectiveness in Early Learning) (DfES, 2002) and Recreating the Reception Year (ATL, 2004).

Introduction

The UK has a long tradition of reflective, play-based practice in early years and infant education which is currently being lost in England in a plethora of prescription. The National Strategies in Literacy and Numeracy have done enormous disservice to the understanding of play because, in practitioners' minds, play is divorced from the required outcomes. Children (and practitioners) have been put under great pressure to reach externally imposed goals: neither children nor adults perform well under pressure because it narrows thinking rather than encourages divergent responses. Young children need to be free from a sense of failure if they are to thrive (Palmer 2007). Play relieves the pressure and is highly effective in generating flexible and creative thinking (Whitebread 2007). Play also generates the concrete experiences which underpin abstract thinking and the ability to use symbols (Bowman et al. 2000). As Elkind (2008) states:

> Play is not a luxury but rather a crucial dynamic of healthy physical, intellectual and social-emotional development at all ages.
>
> (Elkind 2008: 4)

Play deepens children's learning and understanding because it enables them to begin learning from first-hand experiences, based on what they already know and can do (Marton and Booth 1997). As the Early Years Foundation Stage (EYFS) document (DfES 2007) asserts, 'In their play, children learn at their highest level'. However, play does not sit comfortably alongside outcomes-based education because it is open-ended and controlled by the learners. It is therefore a powerful source of evidence for formative assessment. Practitioners need to trust children at play and be aware that observation can help them understand the meanings children are making from their experiences, within and beyond the curriculum. Analysis of children's individual interests and choices provides the evidence base for effective extension of their learning (Rogers and Evans 2008). Confident young players become lifelong learners who are capable of independent, abstract thought, who feel able to take risks in order to solve problems and gain understanding.

We all want our children to achieve, recognising that every child does matter and that their wellbeing is paramount to our future (Every Child Matters, HM Treasury 2004). Regrettably, practitioners in England have been conditioned, by policy requirements and the nature of OFSTED inspections, to engage heavily in adult-directed activities, although these can be shown to limit children's motivation and disposition to learning (Rogers and Evans 2008). The predominance of 'formal' learning activities for young children leaves them little time to develop their understandings of the world through creative and imaginative experiences, the bedrock of quality early years practices (Rinaldi 2005). Policy-makers must have the courage to develop and trust teachers' principled, professional judgements when it comes to dealing with children's individual and unique learning needs as defined in the EYFS. They need also to ensure that training opportunities are available for all early years staff in understanding how to empower, enhance and extend children's learning through self-initiated play experiences.

What actually is play?

It has to be acknowledged at this stage that play has constantly defied all attempts (both practical and philosophical) at definition. Like many innate human processes, play is hard to pin down because it is so varied, flexible and individual to the player(s). What can be described are the behaviours and actions of play and the forms it can potentially take in children's learning and development. Although not perfect, the list given below (a combination of theoretical reading, research and observation over many years) is the nearest we can come to a means of identifying play behaviours:

- Play is intrinsically motivated and self-initiated
- The play process is more important than what it produces
- Everything is possible – reality can be disregarded and imagination allowed to take over
- It is highly creative and flexible
- It is free from externally applied 'rules'
- It has active participation – mind and body
- It has positive, often pleasurable, effects on the player(s)
- The context is open-ended

- The player is deeply involved and committed
- The player has a real sense of decision-making, ownership and control over the play
- The player is self-directed and play often self-initiated.

In other words, in their own powerful play, children are learning many things, including how to:

- be self-motivated, independent, autonomous thinkers
- use their own ideas, thoughts and imagination
- grow in independence of thought and action
- persist and sustain interest
- be confident, competent and able to cope with challenges
- be open-minded, flexible and creative
- be open to exploring, experimenting and investigating new ideas and materials
- acquire and use new knowledge, skills and understandings and much, much more! Readers should feel free to add their own ideas to the list.

Moreover, the Parliamentary Office of Science and Technology Report (2000) concludes that developmental psychology research indicates that children's main sensory, cognitive and linguistic growth is developed through play, exploration, talk and interaction with others rather than with systematic instruction. Hall's (2005: ii) analysis of neuroscience and its contribution to learning asserts that 'neuroscience is confirming ... the importance of emotional engagement in learning', another item to add to the (growing) list above.

Play and policies

Although the word 'play' features in early years documents and policies, it is neither clearly articulated nor well understood by practitioners or policy-makers, particularly in the English context. This became clear in research undertaken by Powell and Wellard (2007: 9). They analysed a sample of 44 English policy documents from 2000 to 2006 and found that there appeared to be 'no single, coherent government message about how play is understood and constructed'. They went on to say that play is also described as 'adult-led' or 'child-initiated' (both of which are tautological descriptions and imply that play can be something other than child-led) or 'free'. The phrase 'learning through planned purposeful play' in the Early Years Foundation Stage (DfES 2007) is perhaps designed to allay adults' fears that young children are not working hard enough. It risks confusing the plans and purposes of adults relating to their goals for children's achievements with the authentic, but different, intentions of playing and playful children.

The implication in many English policy documents seems to be that anything that is undertaken playfully, be that self-initiated activity by the child (see Moyles 2008) or playful teaching by the adults (Moyles and Adams 2001) is sufficient. It does seem that the policy-makers are not prepared to either trust children to learn effectively by their own innate means or to trust adults to understand children's learning through play. Much practitioner education and training is needed to ensure that everyone understands play in children's learning and overall development. Even the flagship Effective Provision of Pre-School Education project (Sylva et al. 2003) hints at practitioners 'using' play for their own ends rather than understanding the power of children's play in generating deeper level learning. Wood (2008) suggests:

> Looking at play only through the lens of defined educational outcomes may result in narrow, literal interpretations, with practitioners failing to understand the symbolic meanings and transformations that occur in play as well as the mythic, magical and metaphorical qualities of play.
>
> (Wood 2008: 10)

All early years educators will empathise with the following statement:

> Play is essential to the healthy development of all children … it contributes to their cognitive, physical, social and emotional wellbeing. Free play is a powerful tool for learning …
>
> (TDA 2007: 2)

Yet the context of this quote is in relation to extended schools and out-of-school activities. This shows, yet again, how play is regularly divorced from 'real' work and learning that takes place, particularly in schools. No wonder then that practitioners themselves find it so difficult to understand and justify play as a powerful basis to their pedagogical practices. It seems accepted that play should be part of extended schools but play in schools and settings – and, I would argue, particularly in Key Stage 1 – is suffering from not being 'trusted' in itself to provide a secure basis for learning and assessment of children's knowledge, skills and understanding. Rather, practitioners are encouraged to utilise play to their own ends to meet children's learning outcomes and, thus, reduce it to what play can be used for, which obscures the essential nature, purposes and complexities of play. This does not only occur in England: American systems often support this approach, which is very different from that advocated by, e.g. both the highly respected Reggio Emilia preschool practices in Italy or the inspirational Te Whāriki curriculum in New Zealand (Papatheodorou 2008).

Current research

As play is so powerful (Elkind 2008) and has now at least been acknowledged in many English government documents and reports – albeit in such an ill-defined manner – it is perhaps surprising that little in-depth research into the processes, behaviours and learning potential of play is currently being funded, at least in the UK. The good news is that there is still research into play being undertaken in the UK and I was fortunate to be part of a group of play scholars who met in April 2008 to examine their current research into play and to consider its implications for practice in the early years of education. The research these individuals have undertaken and interrogated confirms that play is the most powerful medium for learning in the early years. It must not be treated as inferior to teacher-directed activities and has significant implications for the way that adults work best with young children. Some examples are given below.

- Emotional and cognitive development is closely interconnected with play. Children engaged in play situations show greater evidence of problem-solving abilities and creativity. Children engaged in playful tasks they have initiated show higher levels of cognitive self-regulation (Whitebread 2008).
- Children respond positively and quickly when adults convey the acceptance of playful learning in the classroom. Children for whom play is a regular and fulfilling occurrence in the classroom complete teacher-directed tasks more quickly (Howard 2008).
- Social free play is an evolved behaviour and is important for complex, autonomous social behaviour leading to self-knowledge and social competence in both humans and animals. Rough and tumble play experience is essential for children to learn independently the necessary skills to fully engage in the complex social relationships underlying adult society (Jarvis 2008).
- Play promotes the development of conflict resolution skills in young children. Highly social and cooperative play in classrooms has clear links with learning, progression and identity formation (Broadhead 2008).
- Risky play is difficult to theorise but essential for wellbeing. Children need opportunities to push themselves beyond boundaries in familiar environments. Schools and classrooms have become risk-averse places and this is detrimental to children's development and wellbeing (Tovey 2008).
- Children have many ways of making meaning (multi-modality) and this is facilitated through imaginative play. There are clear links between playful meaning-making and the meanings made as they use marks for early writing and for early written mathematics, key aspects of children's learning (Worthington 2008).
- Children's role-play is naturally influenced by the media. This is their culture and should be respected and understood. There are no polar opposites between their online and offline worlds. Motivation for reading/writing is high in virtual worlds, including in social networking sites (Marsh 2008).
- When teachers understand play, its provision and potential, then children respond with multi-narratives and powerful home-school links. Practitioners can and should respect and engage with the uncertainty of play in relation to its inherent learning potential (Goouch 2008).

All of the foregoing leads me to suggest that, in terms of a pedagogy of play, there are certain practices which we must adopt, as practitioners, if we are to sustain our youngest children's innate learning and development potential, which the final section addresses.

Play, learning and teaching

In addition to just being fun, play in all its forms is a powerful scaffold for children's learning: it enables metacognition (learning about how to understand one's own learning and play). It allows children to cope with not knowing something long enough in order to know – they can rehearse, practice, revise, replay and relearn (Moyles 2005). It frees them from worrying about doing things wrong and gives them confidence to try out alternatives. Children learn to establish their own identity and their place in the order of things through play, particularly sociodramatic play and often also in outdoor contexts (Broadhead 2004; Sutton-Smith 2005). Play enables children to interrogate the world in which they find themselves without loss of self-esteem and, above all, play enables children to learn that learning is – and should always be – enjoyable, personally profitable and challenging. This is a vital feature if we are to have happy and well-balanced, flexible learners and citizens of the future. And all this is unique to the individual child.

Perhaps for this reason, it is time to challenge the concept of 'child development' as the basis for early year's pedagogy. Sadly, this is something else that has been hijacked in order to profile 'normal' development as in the English Early Years Profile and the developmental milestones. As anyone who observes children at play will know, children vary in their approaches, capabilities and skills – the enormous variations emphasise how 'unique' each child really is (one key element of the EYFS, DfES 2007). Only observation of their play will show observers what, e.g. individual children bring to their learning, what they already know and can do, how they approach learning and how they interact with others. And this will be different for each child.

It would seem from the current research that there are a few fundamentals (among many others) for educators to adopt in relation to children's play and learning and playful pedagogies:

- Practitioners and policy-makers need an explicit language and a set of shared understandings about what play and learning are about in educational settings.
- Play in all its subtlety is not only an antidote for children being rushed through a curriculum; play *is* the curriculum and not an occasional adjunct.
- Children should be respected and trusted to understand the power of play in their own learning and to take the lead. Practitioners should be respected and trusted similarly to understand children's individual play and learning experiences and potential and to provide an appropriate curriculum and assessment free from prescription.
- Children's social/cooperative play is closely linked to intellectual development and the children's capacity to develop conflict resolution strategies.
- Play supports and develops learning and abstract/symbolic thought in young children. If we have a lot of pressure on us, it actually narrows our thinking

rather than making us divergent thinkers. Play relieves the pressure and is highly effective in generating both abstract and creative thinking.

- Practitioners, researchers, policy-makers and children need to find ways of examining play so that they can connect with each other.
- Early education is about play and playful learning. Practitioners must be supported and educated themselves in an in-depth understanding of play and playful interactions with young children.
- Children want and need to take risks in their play so that they learn how to be safe. We should actively promote policy-makers to understand the need for adventurous play and explore the connections between risky play, risk taking and playing with ideas.
- If we want our children to become independent thinkers, capable of creative problem-solving, then the most powerful medium in which to learn is play.
- Play is a reflection point for all educational activities.
- We need to understand the rich cultural heritages that children bring that become manifest in play, leading to learning. Playful practices must be underpinned by an understanding of each child's own cultural understanding and interests (see, e.g., Brooker 2002).
- Play and playfulness represent a powerful model of flexible human learning which should provide a model for pedagogy.
- Adults who are able to support playful learning are people who are themselves playful.
- Parents need help to understand the power of play as children's main means of learning so that they can be informed about the impact of policies on their children's development.
- Practitioners should make time not only to observe children at play but to listen to the evidence of their learning in play contexts. Only then will they begin to understand the power of play.
- All this demands a highly trained and educated early years workforce. There is a clear need across initial and continuing education courses to re-examine play and pedagogical interrelationships, absolutely crucial in early childhood education.

Concluding remarks

We may only just be beginning to understand what children learn through their play (Elkind 2008; Broadhead et al. 2009 in preparation) but we can clearly see the evidence their play offers for powerful expressions of understanding, enjoyment and dispositions to learning. Anyone who spends time observing children in play contexts and noting how, through actions and words, children are able to give clear indications of prior experiences and learning, will soon be convinced of play's merits for children and the need for practitioners to get to grips wholeheartedly with a powerful – and playful – pedagogy.

References

Bowman, B., Donovan, S. and Burns, M. (eds) (2000) *Eager to Learn: Educating our Preschoolers*, Washington, DC: National Academies Press.

Broadhead, P. (2004) *Early Years Play and Learning: Developing Social Skills and Cooperation*, London: RoutledgeFalmer.

Broadhead, P. (2008) *Conflict and risk-taking in play: bridging home-school cultures*, Play Colloquium paper, Leeds: LMU.

Broadhead, P., Howard, J. and Wood, E. (2009 in preparation) *Play and Learning in Educational Settings,* London: Sage.

Brooker, L. (2002) *Starting School: Young Children Learning Cultures,* Buckingham: Open University Press.

DfES (Department for Education and Skills) (2007) *The Early Years Foundation Stage,* London: DfES.

Elkind, D. (2008) *The Power of Play: How Spontaneous, Imaginative Activities Lead to Happier, Healthier Children*, Cambridge: MA, De Capo Lifelong.

Goouch, K. (2008) *If nobody speaks of remarkable people … understanding teachers who play*, Play Colloquium paper, Leeds: LMU.

Hall, J. (2005) *Neuroscience and Education: A Review of the Contribution of Brain Science to Teaching and Learning*, Glasgow: SCRE Research Report No. 121.

HM Treasury (2004) *Every Child Matters*, London: HM Stationery Office.

Howard, J. (2008) *Understanding children's perceptions of play: implications for learning in the early years,* Play Colloquium paper, Leeds: LMU.

Jarvis, P. (2008) *The bio-cultural roots of play behaviour and its links with social development*, Play Colloquium paper, Leeds: LMU.

Marsh, J. (2008) *Out-of-school play in online virtual worlds and implications for literacy learning*, Play Colloquium paper, Leeds: LMU.

Marton, F. and Booth, S. (1997) *Learning and Awareness*, Mahwah, NJ: Lawrence Erlbaum Associates.

Moyles, J. (2008) 'Empowering children and adults: play and child-initiated learning', in S. Featherstone (ed.) *Bees Not Butterflies*, London: A&C Black.

Moyles, J. (ed.) (2005) *The Excellence of Play*, 2nd edn, Maidenhead: Open University Press.

Moyles, J. and Adams, S. (2001) StEPs: *Statements of Entitlement to Play*, Buckingham: Open University Press.

Palmer, S. (2007) *Detoxing Childhood: What Parents Need to Know to Raise Happy, Successful Children*, London: Orion.

Papatheodorou, T. (2008) 'Exploring relational pedagogy', in T. Papatheodorou and J. Moyles (eds) *Learning Together in the Early Years: Exploring Relational Pedagogy*, London: Routledge.

Parliamentary Office of Science and Technology (2000) *Early Years Learning*, London: House of Commons Education and Employment Select Committee.

Powell, S. and Wellard, I. (2007) *The Impact of National Policies on Children's and Young People's Opportunities for Play*, London: National Children's Bureau/Children's Play Council.

Rinaldi, C. (2005) *In Dialogue with Reggio Emilia: Contextualising, Interpreting and Evaluating Early Childhood Education*, London: RoutledgeFalmer.

Rogers, S. and Evans, J. (2008) *Inside Role-Play in Early Childhood Education: Researching Young Children's Perspectives*, London: Routledge.

Sutton-Smith, B. (2005) *Play: An Interdisciplinary Synthesis*, Lanham, MD: University Press of America.

Sylva, K., Melhuish, E., Sammons, P., Siraj-Blatchford, I., Taggart, B. and Elliot, K. (2003) *The Effective Provision of Pre-School Education (EPPE) Project: Findings from the Pre-school Period*, London: Institute of Education.

TDA (2007) Policy Briefing 2. *Why Play should be a vital element of the extended school 'core offer'*. Online. Available at: http://www.tda.gov.uk/upload/resources/pdf/p.playengland_policybriefing2.pdf (Accessed 8 July 2008).

Tovey, H. (2008) *The dangers of safety: risk and challenge in play outdoors*, Play Colloquium paper, Leeds: LMU.

Whitebread, D. (2007) 'Developing independence in learning', in J. Moyles (ed.) *Early Years Foundations: Meeting the Challenge*, Maidenhead: Open University Press.

Whitebread, D. (2008) *Play, cognition and self-regulation: what exactly are children learning when they play?* Play Colloquium paper, Leeds: LMU.

Wood, E. (2008) *Towards a critical pedagogy of Play*. Play Colloquium paper. Leeds: LMU.

Worthington, M. (2008) *Play is a complex landscape: imagined worlds and possible meanings*. Play Colloquium paper. Leeds: LMU.

Janet Moyles manages, yet again, to remind us all that play is what children do as they seek to make sense of their world and all that is in it. She reminds us to keep children at the heart of learning and development and to ensure that we observe them and listen to them and take seriously what they say and do.

Part II

Understanding children

Everyone who works with children – especially young children – spends a great deal of time observing them as they live and play. Sometimes this observation is casual and provides the observer with some amusing anecdotes about what children say and do. And yet the observation of children is one of the most important tools in the repertoire of any practitioner. Where children are respected as competent beings, practitioners know that in order to enhance children's learning we have to start from where the child is and then plan activities in response to their observed interests and passions and needs. And it is obvious that we can only know where a child is by watching the child, listening to the child and trying to work out what it is that the child is paying attention to. Practitioners are increasingly learning to record what they see and hear and this is important because it ensures that significant moments in learning and development are not overlooked or lost. So practitioners should find ways of recording their observations and use these to plan ahead, and to offer evidence of leaps in learning.

In this part we turn our attention to understanding children.

Chapter 5

Observing symbolic play

Gillian Allery

Gillian Allery, when she wrote this piece, was one of the students on the Early Childhood Studies Scheme at what was the University of North London (UNL). Gillian, like many of the students, was skilled at observing children at play. As one of her assessed assignments, she was invited to observe a child at play and look for evidence of symbolic representation – in other words, to find an example of a child using one thing to represent another. The ability to make one thing stand for another is crucial in early learning. We live in a highly symbolic world. The words we speak, the texts we read, the images we see, the logos we encounter, the numbers we use are all symbols. In order to be able to move away from the here and now and into the abstract world of letters, numbers and symbols, young children need to explore symbolic representation through their play. We were unable to trace Gillian or her fellow students (whose voices you will hear in later parts of the book) but feel sure she and they would be happy for their work to be retained in this second edition. Here, familiar to those who read the first edition, is a wonderful example of a very young child at play. Meet Colin.

I had decided to observe the children outside in the garden and, for a while, I thought it might be a fruitless task, as the children were using things just as they were intended to be used. That is until I saw Colin, aged 2 years, 7 months. Colin went over to the mop bucket outside the kitchen back door. It is a yellow bucket on four wheels. Colin pulled it by the handle away from the door. He pushed it around the garden, quite fast at first, but then slowing to a walk. He stopped, seeing a football on the ground. He picked it up and said 'In you go, baby'. He then pushed the football in the bucket around the garden.

Anabel, aged 4 and a half, came over to Colin. 'Can I have the ball, Colin?'
Colin looked at her. He seemed puzzled. She picked the ball up and kicked it away from her.
'Nooo!' Colin cried and ran after the ball.
One of the workers, Debbie, spoke to Anabel, saying 'Colin is playing with that, Anabel. Come with me and I'll get you another'.

Colin picked up the ball. 'Don't run away, baby. It's all right'. he said lovingly. He then put the ball under his arm and pulled the bucket over to a small chair. He sat down on the chair and put the ball in the bucket. 'Going shops in a minute, baby, shops and sweets, baby, yeah?' he said.

Anabel ran over to Colin. 'Is that a baby, Colin?'

Colin looked pleased. 'Yeah', he replies.

'Can I play?' Anabel asked.

'No pram, you got', Colin said, holding tightly to his bucket. 'I'll get one. Wait, wait there'.

Anabel ran to Debbie. 'Debbie, I need a pram', she said.

Debbie looked around the garden and pointed to a wooden doll's pram standing unused. There you are, Anabel. There is a pram', said Debbie.

'No', said Anabel, 'a yellow one like Colin's please'.

'Oh, a bucket', Debbie said, 'I don't know if we have another one'.

'No, it's a pram, Debbie, one like Colin's got I want', Anabel said indignantly.

'Oh, all right. I'll have a look', said Debbie and taking her by the hand they went inside. Colin, meanwhile, was picking leaves from a bush in the corner of the garden. He carried them carefully back to the bucket/pram and threw them in. 'Dinner, baby', he said.

Pat then called the children for lunch. Colin picked up the ball and went inside.

Pat said, 'Leave that outside, please Colin, till after lunch'.

Colin turned around and ran over to the bucket and put the ball/baby in the bucket and wheeled it into the shade. He patted it and went in for lunch.

Comment on these observation notes

Colin, it seems to me here, is engaging in imaginative play. He uses the bucket as a pram and the ball as a baby. I don't know if Colin saw the ball as a baby or used it as a baby in the absence of a doll. Anabel at first seemed to think Colin's game was silly, but soon engaged in imitative play and decided she, too, wanted a bucket for a pram. The purpose-built pram was rejected as not good enough. Colin uses imitative play when he says 'it's all right' lovingly to the baby after Anabel has kicked it. He also promises the baby a trip to the shops and sweets. It is obvious that he has had some experience of seeing a baby in a pram or indeed it may be the memory of his own pram that has caused him to push the pram out of the sun while he had his lunch. The bucket and ball and leaves are all symbolic representations of something else.

Chapter 6

Under the microscope

Mary Jane Drummond

Mary Jane Drummond has written widely on aspects of early childhood education and is passionate in her belief that it is only through observation that one can know and understand what children can do and are interested in. Some years ago, she was an external examiner for the Early Childhood Studies Scheme at UNL and it was then that she wrote this chapter. When you read it you will see that she has a particular sympathy for and understanding of the learning needs of those working with young children. She read and updated this article and noted, 'As you will see I have made only a few minor adjustments to the main text which I was surprised (and delighted) to find has stood the passing of time rather well! ... I really enjoyed going back to the book and rediscovering its treasures – it was and is a terrific collection of good things'.
Reading this chapter will guarantee that you understand just why observation matters so much.

A 4-year-old girl is looking at a collection of shells, rocks and pebbles untidily arranged on a table, with an assortment of magnifiers of different shapes and sizes. She selects one large spiral shell and examines it closely, first with the naked eye and then with some of the magnifiers. She uses the hand lenses, large and small, moving them to and fro to get the best magnification. She bends down and puts her face right up against the lens, as if she is trying to work out the best distance between her eyes, the lens and the shell. Then she puts the shell down on the table, placing it under a magnifying glass mounted on a tripod; she leans over the tripod, and looks intently at the shell, moving her head up and down, until she seems to be satisfied she has seen all there is to see. She picks up the shell again and holds it to each ear in turn. Then she puts the shell back on the table, under the tripod, and bends over it once more, laying her ear close to the lens, as if she were listening to the shell through the magnifying glass.

This child was not alone with the shells and the lenses. Over in another part of the room, her teacher was working with a small group of her 4-year-old classmates; at a table nearby the teaching assistant was reading a book with two more children. And there was an observer in the room – myself, watching her every move and making copious notes. When I saw her put the shell under the tripod and then lean down to listen to it, I nearly dropped my pen in the excitement of the moment.

Whatever was she doing? Was she ignorant? or stupid? No, neither of these. As I watched, I realised she was asking a question, not out loud, but privately, to herself. She had established that the magnifying glass made the shell look bigger; now she wanted to know 'will it make it louder?'

Isn't that an interesting question for an interested 4-year-old to ask? Doesn't it show us something of how children think? Of course, 4-year-olds don't know as much about the world they live in as we as adults do, but look how they actively explore that world, trying to make sense of it, determined to work out how and why things happen. This young girl was, for those moments, an authentic scientist – generalising, hypothesising and experimenting. And I was lucky enough to be there to see her doing it.

This little incident took place many years ago, but the memory of it is still fresh in my mind – not just because of the girl's original and spontaneous enquiry – but also because of the way in which it so beautifully illustrates everything that is important about observing children.

Watching children – what's in it for us?

All adults who spend time with young children inevitably spend much of that time just watching them. We do so, in part, in the interests of their physical safety; most of us can remember hair-raising incidents when we 'only took our eyes off them for a moment' and when we looked round … disaster! But there's more to watching children than this.

First and foremost, when we watch young children, we can see them learning. And young children's learning is so rich, fascinating, varied, surprising, enthusiastic and energetic, that to see it taking place before one's very eyes, every day of the week, is one of the great rewards of being with young children, as educator, carer or parent. In a sense, watching children is its own justification. It opens our eyes to the astonishing capacity of young children to learn and to the crucial importance of these first few years of our children's lives. But when we watch children we do more than simply marvel at their intellectual and emotional energy; we can also learn, by watching carefully and thinking things over, to understand what we see.

Our own observations can help us understand what the great pioneers of early childhood care and education have taught us about children's learning. Our own observations can illuminate the work of psychologists, researchers and educators. As we watch and listen, their work seems less remote, academic or theoretical: the children bring it to life. As we listen to young children talking, for example, we can understand more clearly the work of Gordon Wells and the Bristol Study 'Language at Home and at School'. His important book *The Meaning Makers* (1987) describes how young children work hard, day after day, at 'making meaning', slowly piecing together their understanding of the puzzling people and things and ideas that make up the exciting world around them. Gordon Wells used expensive radio micro-phones, a large sample of children and a sizeable research team to collect his data; but we can learn about children's talk, about children making meaning, in a more straightforward way, simply by watching and listening attentively. And we can learn for ourselves about what Chris Athey (1990) calls children's 'schematic behaviour', and about what Margaret Donaldson (1978) calls 'disembedded thinking', and about what John Matthews (1994) calls children's 'early mark-making' – we can learn all this, and more, simply by observing children.

An autumn story

One day I was talking to a teacher who seemed to be very agitated and frustrated. She told me about a boy of five she was working with, on a part-time basis, giving indi-vidual support in the classroom, because the educational psychologist had diagnosed him as having special learning difficulties. That diagnosis may or may not have been accurate – but the teacher was certainly having teaching difficulties, and, under-standably perhaps, she was blaming the child. 'He's so ignorant', she told me, 'so deprived and inexperienced. He doesn't know anything'. Thinking this unlikely, I asked her to explain a little – what was the evidence for these alarming charges? 'I'll give you an example', she said. 'He doesn't even know what a conker is!' Since this conversation took place in October, when all over the country children's pockets were full of conkers, I found this story hard to believe and I wanted to know how she knew her pupil didn't know what a conker was. The teacher explained she had shown the boy a conker and asked him what it was. He replied: 'It's an acorn'.

Now, with some genuine, first-hand evidence in front of us, we can start to inter-pret and judge for ourselves. Do you agree with the teacher's verdict? Ignorant? Deprived? Inexperienced? Or do you see something else? Do you see an active learner, an interested enquirer, a meaning-maker? Do you see a child who recognises the object the teacher shows him as the autumnal fruit of a deciduous tree, but who has, in a moment of inattention perhaps, given it the wrong lexical label? Just as we sometimes, inadvertently, say right when we mean left (a mistake which can make quite a difference to a car driver in a busy city centre!).

To say 'acorn', when your teacher expects you to say 'conker', is evidence, as I see it, of both knowledge and experience, combined (unluckily for the child) with nothing more serious than a momentary lapse of memory. Had the child answered at random, uttering words from a totally different area of his experience ('lollipop', say, or 'fire-engine', or 'Mrs Thatcher'), we might have cause for concern. But he didn't. In his search for the name of the object being shown to him, he went, so to speak, to the correct filing cabinet in his mind, opened the right drawer, pulled out the appropriate file – but handed his teacher the wrong sheet of paper.

This small incident too, like the child listening to the shell, made quite an impres-sion on me. It shows how easy it is, unless we guard against it, to look at what chil-dren cannot do, instead of what they can do, at what they do not know, instead of what they know, at what they have not learned, instead of what they are learning at this very minute.

What's in it for the children?

We have seen how observing children, if we do it carefully, attentively, thought-fully, generously, can give us insights into the richness of their learning. There are other important reasons for observing, trying to make sense of what we see: these are to do with the responsibilities of the adults who care for and educate young children. Young children's awesome capacity for learning imposes a massive responsibility on early-years educators to support, enrich and extend that learning. Everything we know about children's learning imposes on us an obligation to do whatever we can to foster and develop it, to provide an environment in which young children's learn-ing can flourish. We cannot know if the environments we set up and the activities we provide for young children are doing what they should, unless we watch care-fully, to keep track of the learning as and when it takes place.

Observing learning, getting close to children's minds and children's feelings, is part of our daily work in striving for quality. What we see, when we look closely, helps us to shape the present, the daily experiences of young children in all forms of early-years provision. The act of observation is central to the continuous process of evaluation, as we look at what we provide and ask: is it good enough?

Our careful observation of children's learning can help us make this provision better. We can use what we see to identify the strengths and weaknesses, gaps and inconsistencies, in what we provide. We can use our observations to move closer to quality provision for all children, and for individuals. We can identify significant moments in a child's learning, and we can build on what we see. If you had observed the child with the shell, how would you take her learning further? What would you bring in for her to explore? A stethoscope? A hearing trumpet? A megaphone? Or other kinds of magnifiers – binoculars or a telescope? Perhaps you would invite her to experiment with the enlarging button on the photocopier; or she might be intrigued by the images of shells thrown on a wall by an overhead projector – she would soon discover how to control the size of the image. Your observation would have helped you to help her – to take her one step further in her exploration of the world and how it works.

And the boy with the conker? What's the next step for him? Further observation, I think, and, preferably out of doors to start with, closer to oaks and chestnuts – and ash trees, sycamores, spindle bushes, sweet chestnuts and privet hedges. Back indoors, he may be intrigued by what's inside these fruits of the hedgerows. You can find out what interests him by watching, trying to understand what he is trying to understand. You can look back, to see what he has already learned; and then look ahead, and see the learning that is just about to take place, in the immedi-ate future. With this understanding, you can be ready to support him and his learn-ing: you can recognise his past achievements, and you can plan for the achievements still to come.

Getting closer to learning

The more closely we watch children, the closer we can come to their learning, their thinking, their questions, their pressing intellectual and emotional concerns. There is a wonderful example of an educator doing just this in Tina Bruce's book, *Time for Play* (1991). A teacher notices an excited group of 4-year-olds causing chaos just out side the home-corner. The noise level is unacceptably high; all the dressing-up clothes are on the floor, and the children are crawling under them, over them and through them. At a moment like this, does a teacher trust children's intellectual strengths? Or call for a return to order? Can an adult believe the children are search-ing for meaning and understanding, when the careful order of the classroom envi-ronment has been so violently disrupted? This teacher did. In a sudden rush of faith and confidence, remembering the 'Peter Rabbit' story she had read them the day before, she realises they are burrowing. When the children confirm her insight, she finds some old sheets, bedspreads and four old clothes' horses, and, with her support, the children soon make a wonderful burrow. They are not in dreadful trouble for infringing classroom regulations: they are free to continue their imaginative play, based on the enclosing/enveloping schema that is the present centre of their interest.

A dear friend and colleague, Annabelle Dixon, an infant teacher whose classroom was a place of genuine intellectual search and discovery, often talked about watch-ing out for 'the grain of children's thinking'. All too often, she used to say, teachers teach across the grain, failing to recognise the children's concerns, pressing on with the prescribed rhythm of the lesson, their learning objectives, the next section of their daily and weekly plans. All too rarely, she argued, do educators take the time to observe, time that will be well spent if it shows them the way that children are going; educators who get close to children's thinking in this way will be well placed to cher-ish and nourish that thinking. Getting close to learning, then, is a worthwhile goal for every educator; but getting close, we must never forget, does not mean taking over. If we set about doing children's thinking for them, pointing out their errors and misjudgements, showing them the proper way to do things, and telling them all the right answers to the problems they set themselves, there will be precious little left for them to do.[1]

For example, a group of young children spent 25 minutes absorbed in water play. The nursery nurse had, at their request, added some blue dye to the water, and the children were intrigued by the different shades of blue they could see: paler at the shallow margin and darker at the deepest, central part of the water-tray. One child was even more interested in another, related phenomenon. He spent nearly 10 min-utes of this period of play observing his own shoes and how their colour appeared to change when he looked at them, through the water and the transparent water-tray. The child seemed to be fascinated by what happened when he placed his feet in dif-ferent positions; he leaned intently over the tray to see what colour his shoes appeared to be at each stage. He did not, of course, use the words 'experiment' or 'observation', but that was what he was engaged in, none the less. After each trial, he withdrew his feet into the natural light of day, as if to check that they retained their proper colour. Had the dye stayed in the water, where he'd seen it put? Or had some of it seeped out, into his shoes?

At the end of the morning session, the teacher and nursery nurse announced that it was time to tidy up. The children worked together to empty the water-tray of the sieves, funnels and beakers they had been using. They took out the jugs, the teaspoons and the ladles, emptied them and put them away. When they had nearly finished, the boy stopped and asked aloud of no-one in particular, 'How do we get the blue out?'

There is, of course, more than one way that an educator could respond to this question. But the one way that will do nothing for the child's learning, or for his understanding, is to tell him that it can't be done, or that he is wrong to even speculate about the possibility. The 'grain' of this child's thinking was running another way. Now the educator's task is not to take over, redirect his thinking, or solve his problem for him. The respectful educator, who is close to his chain of thought (following the grain of his thinking) will, rather, help him plan his next experiments, and the observations that will, finally, satisfy him, that not all changes in colour are reversible (shoes, yes, sometimes; water, sometimes, no).

Conclusion

Glenda Bissex is an American author and educator who, while studying for her master's degree in education, was trying to read one afternoon when her 5-year-old son Paul wanted to play with her. Frustrated in his attempts to make her put down her book, Paul disappeared for a few minutes. When he returned, it was with a piece of paper on which he had printed, with rubber stamps from his printing set, the letters R U D F ('Are you deaf?') His mother was dumbstruck and, in her own words: 'Of course, I put down my book' (Bissex, 1980: 3). From that moment on she added to her academic study of the early acquisition of literacy the daily practice of observing her own son learning to read and write. Her account of what she saw is fascinating reading – not just for its entertaining title 'GNYS AT WRK' (taken from a note Paul pinned on his bedroom door at the age of 5-and-a-half) – but also because of the way she uses her own, personal, first-hand observations, of her own first-born child, to throw light on young children's learning in general.

But she also takes every opportunity to raise difficult and challenging questions about the relationship between teaching and learning. There are passages in her book which make uncomfortable reading for all of us involved with young children's learning; Bissex suggests, gently, but firmly, that all too often children learn in spite of our attempts to educate. She emphasises, as I have tried to do throughout this chapter, the vital importance of listening, watching and waiting, if we are to have any hope of supporting and extending children's learning. In her unforgettable words:

> We speak of starting with a child 'where he is', which in one sense is not to assert an educational desideratum but an inescapable fact: there is no other place the child can start from. There are only other places the teacher can start from.
>
> (Bissex 1980: 111)

Observing children is simply the very best way there is of knowing where they are, where they have been and where they will go next.

Notes

1 I would like to acknowledge here my immense debt to Annabelle Dixon, who tragically died in 2005. Annabelle was an inveterate, indefatigable observer of children, and spending time with her, observing children learning in her classroom, was an education in itself. I learned so much from her about learning. After she left classroom teaching, she collaborated in two projects with which I was also closely involved, Learning without Limits (Hart et al. 2004), and First Hand Experience: what matters to children (Rich et al. 2005). But thousands of teachers, parents and other educators will remember her best, and miss her most, for her penetrating insights into individual children's learning.

References

Athey, C. (1990) *Extending Thought in Young Children*, London: Paul Chapman.

Bissex, G. (1980) *GNYS AT WRK: A Child Learns to Write and Read*, Cambridge, MA: Harvard University Press.

Bruce, T. (1991) *Time for Play*, London: Hodder and Stoughton.

Donaldson, M. (1978) *Children's Minds*, New York: Fontana

Hart, S., Dixon, A., Drummond, M. J. and McIntyre, D. (2004) *Learning without Limits*, Maidenhead: Open University Press.

Matthews, J. (1994) *Helping Children to Draw and Paint in Early Childhood*, London: Hodder and Stoughton.

Rich, D., Casonova, D., Dixon, A., Drummond, M.J., Durrant, A. and Myer, C. (2005) *First Hand Experience: What Matters to Children*, Clopton: Rich Learning Opportunities.

Wells, G. (1987) *The Meaning Makers*, London: Hodder and Stoughton.

Every time I read this chapter it helps remind me to keep my attention on the child, on the learner, and not on any imposed or artificial target or goal. Drummond illustrates so powerfully just what we can learn through really watching children, listening to them, taking an interest in what they are doing and in trying to share their focus of attention. Only by doing this do we really get a window into understanding their learning.

To illustrate this there follows some of the observation notes from the first edition.

Chapter 7

Her eyes are flashing and her ears are sore

Lynne Bennett

Lynne Bennet and **Nancy Coyne** were both students whose work was included in the first edition. We could not trace them to get permission to include their work but feel sure they will be happy to find it here.

Alice (cuddling a pink toy elephant) says, 'This is a sad elephant because its grandma has died. She was getting old'.

Jonathon is cuddling a fluffy yellow duck. He says, 'This is lovely and soft. I'm Batman and I'm going shopping'.

Daniella comes into the house, holding a shopping basket and doll and says, 'Big sister is going shopping and you look after the baby please'. She puts the doll on the sofa and says, 'She is very sick. Put her there [points to a cushion on sofa] and take her hat off. Her eyes are flashing and her ears are sore'. She puts a spoon in the doll's ear and makes the noise 'sloosh, sloosh' and says, 'Now, that's better'. Stands back and looks at the doll and smiles.

Natasha comes over and sits down on a seat in the home corner.

Daniella moves behind her and starts to comb her hair – without asking Natasha.

Daniella says, 'What did your mum say the last time you had your hair combed like that? Did she think it was lovely?'

Natasha replies, 'Well, Stephanie is the dentist and she is going to look at my teeth'. [The dentist had visited us recently.]

Daniella moves over to Alice to give her some medicine and then brush her hair. She says, 'I'm the hairdresser'.

Natasha says, 'I'm going to the ball and I will dance. I don't need anybody – I can dance on my own'.

Daniella has taken a spoon again. She pretends to use the spoon as a torch to look into Alice's eyes. She tells her to blink. Then she says, 'I'm the mummy and I'm off to work. You're the daughter' [points to Natasha]. She takes the telephone and lifts the receiver and says, 'Hello, are you a good girl?'

Natasha lifts the receiver of the other telephone and says, 'Yes, mummy. Bring me some crisps home'.

Comments on this observation

Daniella is aware of different types of sickness and how sick people are treated. She is assertive in using others in her play. The 'sloosh' sound may suggest she has had her ears syringed or used ear drops. She realises medicine is to make people better. You will not be surprised to learn that both her parents are doctors.

What's more, Daniella is interested in initiating role-play. She pays attention to detail regarding sickness. Her vocabulary indicates knowledge in this area. She concentrated on making the patient better and was pleased with herself for doing so.

Chapter 8

Louise drawing

Nancy Coyne

Louise picks up a green pen and starts to draw zigzags on the paper.

Nancy: That looks interesting.
Louise: I'm drawing stairs.
Nancy: Oh, let me see how you draw stairs.
Louise: It's very easy. You just go up and down, up and down, like this.

She was nodding her head up and down at the same time.
She drew a circle and then began to scribble around it.

Louise: I'm doing long hair all the way round. Look at the person I did.
Nancy: Oh, that's lovely. Is it anybody I know?
Louise: Me, silly! Can't you tell by the hair?
Nancy: Oh, silly me!
Louise: I think I'll draw four people because I am four.
Nancy: That's a good idea.
Louise: I'll make them all hold hands.
Nancy: Are they playing a game?
Louise: Yes, Ring-a-Ring of Roses. I'll do black for a boy because black is a boy's colour. I don't like black. Do you?
Nancy: I like black clothes.
Louise: You should be a boy then. [Laughs]
Nancy: Cheeky girl!
Louise: Next is yellow for a girl.
Nancy: That's a nice bright colour.
Louise: Yes, that's why I like it. It's the same colour as the sun.
Nancy: That's right.
Louise: Do you like them all holding hands? They are at a birthday party, so I'll give the special one a crown so we'll know whose birthday it is.
Nancy: I think that's a very good idea.
Louise: Another boy and then a girl. I have to give them all a name now.

She points to each one and names them – Roger, Sina, Bana, Keiren, Mark, Keiren again.

Nancy: They are nice names.
Louise: Now I'm going to give them all a nose.
She bangs the pen hard at each face to give them each a nose.
Louise: How do you spell Ring-a-Ring a Rosies?

I spelled out each letter and she wrote them down with her tongue between her teeth. Then she wrote her age and her name.

Nancy has recorded what she saw and heard and also recorded her own responses. What I like is how she accepts whatever the child does and says and doesn't intervene in order to 'teach' the child anything.

In terms of understanding and explaining what we see individual children doing, a useful technique is to look for evidence of children following particular themes in their play. You will remember Mary Jane Drummond above talking about how observation can help us know more about the particular schemas (or repeated patterns of behaviour) that children are following. The term 'schemas' comes from the work of Piaget and recent research by Chris Athey (1990) has shown how an understanding of these behaviours – often seen as random – can give another view of children's particular enthusiasms and concerns.

Chapter 9

Patterns of play

Observing and supporting young children's schemas

Fran Paffard

Fran Paffard, in this chapter, draws on her considerable experience as a nursery teacher and on the work she was doing in this field for an MA. This chapter, written while the author was Deputy Headteacher of an inner London nursery school, explains how an understanding of schematic behaviour can influence perceptions of children and also explains how those of us working with young children can use evidence of schemas in order to plan for progression.

I was first introduced to the idea of using schemas in early years education while re-training as a nursery teacher at the Froebel Institute, where Chris Athey (1990) and Tina Bruce (2005) undertook their initial research. Going back to the nursery, I began to look at children's play with new eyes. What had previously appeared to me to be random, aimless behaviour now emerged as a part of the child's exploration of a particular form or 'schema', e.g. Quyen walked around with books up her jumper; she buried animals in the sand; she built boxes from polyhedrons and put dinosaurs in them; she did beautiful drawings then folded them up and put them in her coat pocket; at story time she always sat under the table. Instead of seeing this as pointless and slightly frustrating behaviour, I could now see it as a part of an enveloping schema.

What is a schema?

The word schema can sound like off-putting jargon, but getting to grips with schemas can extend our understanding of how children are actually learning. The word 'schema' comes from the work of Piaget. He saw children's learning as a process moving from actions through to thought. The child, by repeating patterns of actions, is both learning to generalise (e.g. which objects are suckable) and assimilating those experiences into this pattern (e.g. dummies are suckable, coal isn't). These are the patterns of action he called schemas. A schema then is simply a 'pattern of repeatable behaviour'.

Chris Athey and Tina Bruce, observing 3- and 4-year-olds in a nursery setting, found that they were engaging in 'patterns of repeatable behaviour' or 'schemas' that clearly influenced their learning. It is this research which has motivated early years practitioners to find out how schemas can help in their work. Schemas are fundamentally biological in form with sociocultural content (Bruce 2005). Thus, through a child's schema they explore and assimilate new experiences and make sense of their world.

Athey suggests that there are four main ways in which a schema shows itself:

1   Sensory/motor
2   Symbolic/representational
3   Functional dependency
4   Thought.

Consider Sophie, below, who, at the age of three, demonstrated her absorption in rotation and a connected circular schema in all these modes.

Sensory/motor

Sophie spent lots of time outside in the nursery, chasing round and round the trees, riding round the edge of the tarmac on a bike and spinning around on an old tyre swing. Given a skipping rope, she didn't skip, but spun around so that the rope flew out in a wide circle. In the corn flour tray, she used both hands to form wide circles.

Symbolic/representational

Sophie loves the workshop, sticking tissue paper circles together and selecting round plastic lids and corks to use. Her paintings were all of circles, lollipops, suns, flowers and if there was a choice of painting paper she always chose the circles. She enjoyed Plasticine and loved rolling it into balls and sausage shapes. Shopping with her mother, she insisted on buying turkey roll 'because I only like the circle ones'.

Functional dependency

Sophie explores the cause and effect of her schema, she used the model clock in the playhouse shop moving the hands to different points 'now the shop is open, now it is closed time'. She spent happy times in the washroom turning the taps on and off and watching as the turning motion controlled the flow of water.

Thought

With blocks, Sophie chose a cylindrical block and rolled it down the ramps, she showed another child how to position the block 'or it won't go down properly'. When we lost the marbles for the marble run, Sophie made some balls from Plasticine, experimenting to get them the right size 'they have to be really round to go down'.

In all these different modes Sophie was obviously interested in *circularity* and *rotation*. Her interest led her to explore her own body movements and the movements of objects. It led her into modelling and artwork, into trying to represent her experience in a symbolic way. And it led her into hypothesising, making conceptual deductions about circles, spheres and cylinders. She explored ideas of time, forces, propulsion and one-to-one correspondence, to name only a few. It was obvious watching her that she was very absorbed in her explorations and was gaining deep satisfaction from her learning. At the same time, she was able to communicate her ideas and cooperate with other children. Athey suggests that through schemas, we are able to understand and therefore assist the progression from action to thought for the young child. What began for Sophie as a chasing game in the nursery garden resulted in all kinds of valuable learning across the range of nursery provision.

How many schemas are there?

It can be hard to provide a definitive list of schemas. Each schema connects to and builds on a child's existing schemas, e.g. a child explores vertical and horizontal schemas before she or he can explore a grid or a cross schema. Children may be exploring a variety of schemas at one time, or a child's schema may not be easy to observe, so we need to be wary of over-simplifying the way in which they work. However, various lists have been produced of some identifiable schemas in children's play and I am including here a list based on the Rumpus Schema Extra produced by Cleveland teachers in early education. This is a list I have found useful as a starting point with early years practitioners and parents in introducing schemas.

A schema spotter's guide

Transporting

A child may move objects or collections of objects from one place to another perhaps using a bag, pram or truck.

Positioning

A child may be interested in placing objects in particular positions, e.g. on top of something, around the edge, behind. Paintings, models and buildings show evidence of this.

Orientation

This schema is shown by interest in a different viewpoint, as when a child hangs upside down.

Dab

A graphic schema used in paintings randomly or systematically to form patterns or to represent, e.g. eyes, flowers, buttons, etc.

Trajectory

A fascination with things moving or flying through the air: balls, aeroplanes, frisbees, etc. When expressed through the child's own body movements this often becomes kicking, punching, jumping or throwing.

Horizontality and verticality

A child may show evidence of particular interest by actions such as climbing, stepping up and down or lying flat. These schemas may also be seen in constructions, collages or graphically. After schemas of horizontality and verticality have been explored separately, the two are often used in conjunction to form crosses or grids. These are very often systematically explored on paper and interest is shown in everyday objects, such as cooling trays, grills, nets, etc.

Diagonality

Usually later than the previous schemas, this one emerges via the construction of ramps, slides, and sloping walls. Drawings begin to contain diagonal lines forming roofs, hands, triangles, zigzags.

Enclosing

A child may build enclosures with blocks, Lego, large crates, etc. perhaps naming them boats, ponds and beds. The enclosure is sometimes left empty, sometimes carefully filled in. An enclosing line often surrounds painting and drawings while a child is exploring this schema.

Enveloping

This is often connected to enclosure. Objects, space or the child herself are completely covered. She may wrap things in paper, enclose them in pots or boxes with covers or lids, wrap herself in a blanket or creep under a rug. Paintings are sometimes covered over with a wash of colour or scrap collages glued over with layers of paper or fabric.

Circularity

Circles appear in drawings and paintings as heads, bodies, eyes, ears, hands, feet, etc. They are also used in representing animals, flowers, wheels, the sun, and a wide variety of other things.

Semi-circularity

Semi-circles are also used graphically as features, parts of bodies and other objects. Smiles, eyebrows, ears, rainbows and umbrellas are a few of the representational uses for this schema as well as parts of letters of the alphabet.

Radial

Again common in paintings and drawings. Spiders, suns, fingers, eyelashes, hair, often appear as a series of radials, clocks will show radials turning inwards. Play dough cakes have lots of candles sticking up.

Rotation

A child may become absorbed by things which turn, e.g. taps, wheels, cogs, keys. She may roll cylinders along, or roll herself. She may rotate her arms or construct objects with rotating parts in wood or scrap materials.

Connection

Scrap materials may be glued, sewn, fastened into lines; pieces of wood are nailed into long connecting constructions. String, rope, wool, etc. are used to tie objects together, often in complex ways. Drawings and paintings sometimes show a series of linked parts. The opposite of this schema may be seen in separation where interest is shown in disconnecting assembled or attached parts.

Ordering

A child may produce paintings and drawings with ordered lines or dabs; collages or constructions with items of scrap carefully glued in sequence. She may place blocks, vehicles or animals in lines and begin to show interest in 'largest' and 'smallest'.

One-to-one correspondence

There is often evidence of this in scrap collages and constructions where a child may, e.g. glue a button inside each bottle top or place a piece of paper inside each cup of an egg box.

Functional dependency

Although causal relationships are not fully appreciated, interest may be seen in the dependency of one function upon another, e.g. a child may draw a lift with a button beside it and say, 'You have to press this button for the lift to come', or pretend to turn an ignition key 'so that the engine will start'.

Schemas cluster

Some children are clearly in a dominant schema. This can be particularly obvious when watching children under 3 years; the toddler who determinedly 'posts' everything into the bin, through the letterbox or down the back of the radiator. Often however, children will be involved in a cluster of schemas, exploring and coordinating their learning through a cluster of interrelated schemas. Douglas loved cars and followed his interest in spinning the wheels, cars in tunnels and garages, and long lines of cars, clustering rotation, enveloping and horizontal schemas all through the medium of his fascination with cars.

Why look at schemas?

Looking at schemas reinforces some basic principles of early childhood education.

1   It is child-centred and positive. Looking at a child's schema involves starting from where the child is and what the child can do, not what she cannot.
2   It is easy to make assumptions about children's capabilities. Schema-spotting helps to avoid these judgements since it depends on close observation. A child who is thought to have a short concentration span because they flit from place to place may be found to be continuously exploring an idea or schema across different areas.
3   It encourages us to respect the child's interests and enables workers to interact with the child in a more helpful way. A child who is in a 'transporting schema' and takes all the home corner cups and plates to the far end of the garden can be given a picnic set to use.
4   Behaviour perceived as negative may be understood to be part of a schema, so that children are not automatically labelled as naughty and their behaviour can be channelled into more acceptable routes. Danny, who was constantly in trouble for kicking and knocking over children's buildings was as relieved as I was when we gave him his own pile of crates to kick and skittles to knock over.
5   Although schemas and their categories can sound off-putting and full of jargon, I have found that talking to parents about their child's schemas is a very helpful way of working together. One worker cannot possibly track a class full of children, but parents are acute observers of their children and are quick to spot changes in the patterns. It also helps parents to share in their child's learning. One patient mum received a soggy folded piece of painted paper with delight every day for a whole term, respecting her daughter's enveloping schema and gave her paper, paints and masking tape to let her carry on at home.
6   As adults, we bring to young children the vocabulary and the categories we grew up with. Learning is categorised into subjects (science, history, etc.) and social and emotional behaviour is seen as a separate issue. Schemas, once the initial terminology is understood, provide a new and generally positive way of

interpreting the child's actions, in which learning and behaviour are closely enmeshed.

7   Recognising a schema can help us to predict and to offer the kinds of experiences that will extend a child's learning. Tina Bruce suggests that we can both broaden a schema by offering a range of content to fit the form of the schema, or that we can seek to deepen a schema, offering experiences or interactions that seek to deepen the child's developing conceptual understanding of the schema. So a child in a grid schema may be interested in maps, in peg boards, in windows, in weaving. A child who uses only limited areas of the nursery may be lured into using others by giving her, e.g. squared paper in the graphics area, blocks to build with, a crossroads for toy cars or trains, long thin strips of card or wood and nails, staples, glue for fixing them, or the task of cutting up a tray of biscuits into squares.

Supporting schemas

If we look at the usual areas of early years provision with schemas in mind, new priorities emerge:

Materials

Do we provide circles, squares, grids, oblongs, etc. in the paper rack? Does the home corner have blankets, bags, mixing bowls for enclosers and envelopers? Is there equipment outside for transporting: trolleys, wheelbarrows, rucksacks, etc.? Ropes and string for connecting? Balls and skittles for throwing and rolling? Hoops and old tyres for rolling and spinning? Ideally, all areas should provide for all schemas, and obviously the more open-ended the provision the better. Masking tape and paper bags are far more versatile than expensive toys from catalogues.

Rules

Allowing children freedom to explore their schemas is crucial. A child in a dynamic vertical schema probably won't be interested in a butterfly printing activity, but will they be allowed to do the splash paintings they enjoy instead? Do we allow children to fold up their paintings, to wrap things up in masking tape, to carry around shopping bags, to take things from inside out – or provide alternatives outside? This does not mean that we shouldn't plan to introduce new and stimulating ideas into the nursery, but as staff we need to be ready to follow the child's interests and not try to impose the learning we have so carefully provided.

Interactions

Do we value the action part of a schema, and see the child who is zooming cars across the carpet as just as busily learning as the child producing lots of drawings? Do we talk to children about what they are doing and listen to them, acknowledging their interest and feeding in the language to support it? Are we ready to feed and deepen the *form* of the schema, as well as to broaden the possible *content*? Do we make connections, suggest other things to look at? Read stories that support their schemas? Do we talk to parents about their child's pattern of play and ask about how they play at home?

Planning

- Planning for schemas in the early years doesn't cancel the need for other forms of planning, but it can incorporate planning from children's interests.
- Plan the nursery environment so that each area has basic provision for common schemas.
- Plan specific activities, outings and experiences with particular schemas and children in mind.
- It is not possible to plan for every child all the time, but possibilities include: (a) allowing staff observation time for key children, to identify and support their schemas; (b) focusing on one schema and providing for it in detail for 1 week; (c) tracking certain children, identifying schemas and recording the learning going on; (d) making the tracking of a child's schema a regular part of whatever record keeping is being done.

A warning

Not every child is easily identified as being involved in a schema, some may be involved in two or three at once, others may not seem to be particularly immersed in any. Schema-spotting, fascinating though it is, should not become an exercise in 'labelling' children. Its usefulness lies in illuminating the child's inner learning, focusing us more clearly on what children are doing, not trying to fit their behaviour into boxes. Identifying a child's schema is only one of many tools at our disposal in observing and supporting children's learning. It is also easy to forget that children move between schemas, sometimes overnight. Thinking that you know a child's schema does not mean that you can stop observing, or that you can make assumptions about them. I have also heard some schemas being characterised in a negative way, e.g. the trajectory or dynamic vertical schema being associated with throwing, kicking and destructive behaviour. Schemas can help us to understand and channel some difficult behaviour certainly, but every schema has crucial learning embedded in it which needs to be supported and valued.

Finally, I would only add that research on schematic learning in children is not particularly widespread. There is much that we still do not know about them. The more early years practitioners critically explore the possibilities of schemas, the more we shall find out.

Acknowledgement

This chapter is particularly indebted to Tina Bruce whose definitive early years text, *Early Childhood Education*, 3rd edn. (London: Hodder and Stoughton 2005) has an essential chapter on schemas.

Further reading

Athey, C. (1990) *Extending Thought in Young Children*, London: Paul Chapman.
  A fascinating, but quite difficult account of her research.
Bruce, T. (2005) *Early Childhood Education*, 3rd edn.London: Hodder and Stoughton.
  Includes an essential chapter on schemas.
Nicholls, R. (ed.) with Sedgwick, J., Duncan, J., Curwin, L. and McDougall, B. (1986) *Rumpus Schema Extra: Teachers in Education,* Cleveland: Cleveland LEA.
  A practical basic pamphlet for nursery workers and parents.
Nutbrown, C. (1994) *Threads of Thinking*, London: Paul Chapman.
  An accessible read, looking at using schemas in early education.
Whalley, M (2007) *Involving Parents in Their Children's Learning*, London: Paul Chapman.

In order to understand children we need to try and understand what it is that they are paying attention to. What questions are they asking implicitly as they play and explore, draw and paint, sing and dance, look and listen? What small theories are they developing through this looking and listening and taking part and being alone? Mary Jane Drummond gives us the suggestion that it is only by observing children that we can know not only where they are but where they have been and where they are going. She follows in the tradition of great educators like the legendary Susan Isaacs. Fran Paffard takes us into the sometimes strange worlds of children following their passions and developing them in many and various ways in order to make sense of aspects of the world that interest or concern them. Her work and that of people like Cathy Nutbrown and Chris Athey help us understand behaviours that might appear random and haphazard.

Part III

All our children

Over the years since the publication of the first edition, much has changed. Patterns of strife and war and discrimination and economic boom and bust have uprooted whole populations, increased the numbers of people having to leave their own countries to seek a life elsewhere, made some of the wealthy decide that one home in the home country is not enough and so on. Cities and towns in the developed world are filled with an undreamed-of wealth and variety of cultures and languages. Many children now take it for granted that English is not the only language; white not the only skin colour. There are advantages and disadvantages. Many immigrant children still suffer discrimination, are still neither seen nor heard, and have negative comments made about them and their lives. In law, there have been changes too.

The publication of the first edition of this book came soon after the election of New Labour in 1997 and it was disappointing for many in education to see policy development closely mirroring that of the previous conservative government. The aim was to raise standards in literacy and numeracy and you will know how that resulted in the development of the daily Literacy Hour in English and Welsh primary schools. Whole class teaching and the splitting up of children into 'ability' groups became the norm. It was the start of the testing and measuring culture which is still with us and still determining the daily experiences of our children.

With the change of century a new dimension appeared in the debates around language teaching. Now, based on recommendations from the National Languages Steering Group, the National Languages Strategy (DfES 2002) stated that all primary school children should learn another language in order that closer links between diverse communities be established, but the rhetoric of doing this has come to little. There are however, some glimmers of light – Excellence and Enjoyment: A Strategy for Primary Schools (DfES 2003), which is part of the Primary National Strategy, recommends both close working with parents and the community and thinking beyond the traditional school day. Every Child Matters (DfES 2003) promotes a multidisciplinary approach to the care and education of all children and young people in the age range from birth to 19 years. This document cites Section 10 of the Children Act 2004 which places the duty on local authorities and their partners to pay attention to improving the wellbeing of all these children and young people and makes reference not only to the statutory sectors but also to voluntary and community organisations. Similar aims are set out in a range of documents (e.g. Aiming High: Raising Attainment for Minority Ethnic Pupils, DfES 2003). And finally, recent teaching materials, arising out of the PND/EAL pilot project (NALDIC, 2004) and directed at both literacy and EAL consultants, offer the possibility of bilingual pedagogies in primary school.

This is an important section of the book and some of what you read will be familiar to those of you who knew the first edition. It has two key chapters, one updated by Birgit Voss, and one specially commissioned for this book and written by Charmian Kenner.

Chapter 10

Supporting young children

Birgit Voss

Birgit Voss was a nursery school teacher, when this chapter first appeared, working in a nursery class in inner London. She herself is bilingual and she has spent most of her working life considering the particular needs of young bilingual children and those of their parents. Anyone visiting her classroom was immediately aware that this was a very mixed group of children in terms of language, culture, gender, ability and class. The resources, the activities and the images all reflected this. When asked to review her chapter in 2008, Birgit was the head of Andover Early Years' Centre where a lot of the 'thinking' evident in the chapter you are about to read has been put into practice. Invited to review and update her chapter for this second edition Birgit decided that it could stand, relatively unchanged and said, 'What I said way back then is still valid and still constitute guiding principles for my work today'.

So here we are, Autumn 1994. A new term has begun and I have just finished the first week. What have we got in my class for the next 4 months? Who are these children that I am supposed to teach according to their needs and interests, taking into account the individual experience they bring to school? When I say 'I', I don't mean 'I' alone. Actually, there are quite a few others involved in the 'delivery of the curriculum, providing a safe, happy and stimulating environment for all our pupils' (to quote OFSTED). There is Jean, the Nursery Nurse, and two Primary Helpers, who cover for our breaks. There is the lunchtime helper, our Section 11 teacher (unfortunately, we only enjoy her company for one term. Next term, she will take our transferring children up to the summer reception class which now starts after Christmas.) There is also my co-teacher who takes the class 1 day a week – I work 4 days per week. The headteacher comes to read a story once a week and we always have a number of students/visitors. Therefore 'I' am the leading member of quite a large team, which is trying to deliver our Early Years Curriculum. We all have different viewpoints, different strengths and values, different levels of awareness, different educational backgrounds (and different salaries!). Our teaching staff is entirely female, which most certainly has a limiting effect on some of our pupils, since we are able to offer no male role models. In 1982 in inner London, there were 12 male nursery teachers out of a total of 600. We may express our aims differently. I might say,

'I try to ensure that each child has equal access to all areas of the curriculum. I know the forces and pressures of racism, sexism, class bias, able-bodiedism, ageism – and possibly other oppressive systems based on prejudice – might have a negative effect on our pupils' learning and wellbeing and may hold them back from fulfilling their whole potential'.

Jean, on hearing this would probably look to the heavens and, with a sigh of exasperation, say, 'Oh, Be, what does that mean? Such jargon! How can our parents understand that? Can't we talk proper English with one another?' She has a point, of course, but Germans like me simply like to make long sentences! And the whole team would certainly agree that we all want our pupils to be happy.

So what have we got then, this term and how can we ensure that they are all happily learning? For the first 2 weeks of term we have only the 18 children who were part-time last term. Twelve stay for lunch; six go home and return afterwards. We have facilities to ensure a high quality lunchtime for 12 children only. Six children sit with a member of the team at each of the two tables and lunch is, of course, not simply about food intake. All areas of the curriculum can be covered in that single hour. It is often the right time for 'intimate' conversations and children have shared many family secrets, joys and pleasures and things that trouble them.

We already know these 18 children quite well. Four girls and 14 boys. Why do I get a slight sinking feeling looking at this distribution? Help! So many boys, such imbalance! Is this my sexism speaking? My fear of the many Batmans and Captain Scarletts trying to kill each other constantly, brandishing swords and pointing guns made from anything at all – stickle bricks, pencils, blocks, straws – noisy behaviour, looking so much more competitive and combative? Looking more closely, I reassure myself that some of these 14 boys actually don't like rough and tumble noisy play. It is more natural to them to do things quietly and gently. So there is some hope. And one of the girls has to be watched; she can be quite spiteful and vicious to others. Still, there is a better class dynamic when the boy/girl ratio is more even. It will get slightly better when our part-timers join us. Then we will have 33 children in all, more boys than girls, 16 bilinguals (five at the beginning stages of English), one boy with speech problems, another with behaviour that borders on autism. I wonder if we should get the Educational Psychologist in to observe him.

Even although we know some of these children very well already, it is always surprising how one's expectations have to be adapted. Young children change at a fantastic rate and they often behave very differently when they start coming full-time. I consider it one of the beauties of our work: it's always full of surprises! The long summer holiday emphasises the changes. Some of our pupils have changed in appearance – different hair, grown taller, they use words with greater sophistication, have grown more confident. Some have become more attached to their parents and a previously happily settled boy is showing unexpected depths of rage, anger and upset at his mother's leaving. He is also using English now as though it was his first language (which is, in fact, Urdu). Yet another little girl who simply couldn't settle last term and whose piercing howls disrupted school life for weeks now smiles sweetly at her dad and with excited chatter in Bengali takes her leave from him. She takes Jean's hand, looks at her with big, trusting eyes, smiles again, gets a little cuddle and I am amazed once again. No tears at all? Yes, it is possible. Even the children we think we know very well we have to observe carefully again, make our mental notes about their progress and changes and, at the end of the day, when the last child has finally gone (usually picked up late), Jean and I swap our notes. At this stage we only record our observations verbally. Later on, when we have collected more data we will commit something to paper. Each child has a record where we enter relevant changes and collect samples of work.

This record is usually started at the home visit. It is an adapted version of the Primary Learning Record which is used by the other classes in our school (and popular before the introduction of the literacy strategy) and parents help me to fill in the first page. It is our policy that each child gets this opportunity to meet me in the safety of her/his home environment. Last term, because of our continuous cuts in funding, the headteacher had to cover for my visits – an indication of how important we think this first home school link is. This term, the Section 11 teacher will cover for my visits.

I usually take a puzzle, a book, some drawing material and a photo book with pictures of the team, the school, our class and the children at work. We look through this book together, often with grandparents, aunts and uncles, as well as parents and the child and siblings. I chat a bit about the kind of things children can do in our class. The pictures speak for themselves when I am unable to communicate in the family's language. That, and a great deal of body language, smiles and gestures, usually gets the message across.

During the visit, I also take some photographs of the child. They are used later when the child comes to school to mark her/his space on the coat hooks, the towel hook and the third, whole body one, for the magnet board. The home visit is a good opportunity to ask the parents to write their child's name in the family's language. I usually let them write it into the record. From there I can enlarge it on the photocopier at school and use it in our graphics area and anywhere else where the child's name appears in English. A very easy way to get dual language writing samples!

When these children join us (we admit one per session for about 2 weeks, starting during the third week of term) the often painful process of separation is facilitated by having met me and having talked about the visit with the parents. Naturally, we do encourage parents to stay with their child as long as we think necessary.

From my home visits I know that some of the bilingual children joining us are very much at the beginning stages of learning English. I make a note of the different languages our little community will be using for the next 4 months: Gujerati, Bengali, Turkish, Urdu, Cantonese, Persian, Arabic, German and, of course, English. I check these against our present resources. We have cassette and video story tapes in all the languages but Cantonese. We have plenty of writing samples, newspapers and magazines in Chinese as we had some Chinese-speaking children earlier. When we celebrated Chinese New Year, we stocked up during a visit to the local Chinese supermarket. We also have appropriate clothes, fabrics and home base equipment – and lots of pictures. The parents seemed very open, friendly and cooperative during the home visit. I am sure they would love to make some story tapes, maybe some songs for us – something to organise.

For the other bilingual children we probably, at this stage, do not need to prepare anything different from what we normally offer. The way children learn in our class by firsthand experience, building on and extending what they already know, is ideally suited to acquiring another language. Children are encouraged to collaborate with each other and research has shown that bilingual children working and learning with their English-speaking peers get to know English very fast. We provide many opportunities for rehearsal and repetition of natural language patterns and, of course, we have many stories with additional visual support (things like story props, either two or three-dimensional). The team is aware that often children in the beginning stages of learning English go through the 'silent period'. This is a time when data is collected and processed. They need to listen, observe and feel confident before they dare to utter the first English word. Bombarding them with direct questions and insisting on a response can be very intimidating during this time. How often do we teach by asking questions? Even I, who through my own experiences am very aware of this silent period phenomenon (I didn't dare speak an English word for nearly a whole year when I first came to this country!), catch myself asking silly questions, but having done so also provide the answer and do not expect it from the child. There are many opportunities in a busy nursery classroom in which spoken English is not a requirement for participation in an activity.

For example, there is the use of the magnet board. This is used for story props but also the photo cut-outs and names. The photo cut-outs consist of a full-length portrait of the child cut out and covered in clear, self-adhesive film. A piece of magnetic tape is stuck to the back, which then sticks the picture onto anything metal. Often children, in groups or alone, arrange and re-arrange these figures, inventing their own stories or re-enacting familiar ones. They also get arranged according to friendship patterns. Occasionally, one 'disappears' under the carpet or attempts are made to bite somebody's head off. I much prefer this aggression to be played out on the symbolic level than on the real person. A photo can be replaced!

The photo cut-outs have the potential to reflect the whole class community: big and small, staff and pupils, all have their miniature reflections there. Like the mirrors we also have in our classroom, they confirm immediately that everybody has their place in our class – everybody belongs. One's image is present, reflected and valued. This is part of our ethos. We try to represent in the classroom, through pictures, fabric, imaginative play materials, puzzles, dolls and books, all our children's and staff's different cultures. We have a number of small saris, Chinese jackets, chopsticks. We have photos of daddies changing nappies and bottle-feeding babies. There are pictures of women car mechanics, a woman 'milkman'. Our reception classes and our class have chosen the topic 'water' to work through until half-term. (In our school we plan together in year groups.) We have pictures of Indian women washing their clothes in the river; of African women carrying babies on their backs and water/food on their heads. We have photographs of male and female fire-fighters on the wall, etc. The most important resource is, however, the children and their work. They provide endless opportunities for extension and reflection. I use photography a great deal, despite the lack of money. The school cannot pay for this expense any longer, so now the cost is covered by the class fund, i.e. parental support. Each child has three places, as a rule, where their photo is displayed. Additionally, I have illustrated many daily routines and sequenced activities, e.g. we put out our toothbrush, go to the loo, wash our hands and sit down. This also has a little song. Things like finger painting, cooking, being outside, working in the garden, playing with water, looking after babies – anything at all can be extended further by making a little book and keeping it as a record. This is a valuable way of introducing literacy within a relevant, meaningful context.

The needs of bilingual children and beginner readers are similar, when it comes to book making. Both groups benefit from repetitive language patterns, easy and clear texts in different contexts with obvious clues to meaning. We have many, many photo books with very simple texts or captions. With some help from the parents, these can easily become dual-text books.

A further check through my records on newcomers reveals another gap in our resources. A little boy will join us whose family consists of two mothers and a brother. We have nothing at all to reflect homosexual relationships in our class. How can I validate his experience? And will I break some sort of law if I do so? Well, if I do then good teaching is probably illegal. And I do think that homophobia is one of 'the other oppressive systems based on prejudices which might have a negative influence on our pupils' learning and wellbeing and hold them back from fulfilling their whole potential'. Luckily I noticed that Letterbox Library have a book among their stock list which depicts a lesbian relationship. It's called Asha's Mums. I do trust Letterbox Library's judgement. Their books are carefully selected and screened. When this little boy and his mums come to our school they will find this book prominently displayed on the shelves and they can feel accepted. I am looking forward to this term. It feels like it might be very stimulating and exciting. I just hope that I can stand the pace. Luckily we will be able to do a great deal more, thanks to the input of our Section 11 teacher. She has already made us a number frieze in Urdu, Bengali, Cantonese and English, using photographs of the children. And we are planning little outings with small groups and turn-taking games. We will be able to give more individual attention when listening to story tapes, and, having additional staff, we might try exciting recipes (maybe something Chinese or Indian) for our cooking session. We will be able to shop for the ingredients with the children beforehand – very good!

If we are even more fortunate, perhaps the Turkish/Bengali mother-tongue teachers (appointed by our Education authority) will be allocated to our school and work with us for a few sessions. We have to be grateful for little crumbs nowadays. In Sweden, it is a child's statutory right to be taught in her/his mother tongue. Would that be too expensive? My guess is that it would cost half of the amount the Government has recently spent in all, introducing and changing the National Curriculum.

It is useful to learn a few words – maybe greetings – in all the languages of the children. We have these written up in the book corner and send the children home with a greeting in their home language. The Language Census of 1986 revealed that, in London schools, 172 different languages were spoken. That means that one-quarter of all pupils have a home language other than English. The most frequently spoken language in 1987 was Bengali, followed by Turkish, Chinese, Gujerati, Urdu, Spanish, Punjabi, Arabic, Greek, French, Yoruba, Portuguese, Italian and Vietnamese. Under the Inner London Education authority this diversity was recognised and provision was made for it. For two years I worked for a team which specialised in making people working with young children aware of the needs of bilingual pupils. Many new resources were created by this team and we worked out a set of beliefs that guided our work. These beliefs, quoted by Liz Finkelstein in an article called 'Some Children in my Nursery Don't Speak English' (1990) still hold true today:

1   Language issues must be tackled in the context of equality of opportunity and with particular reference to issues of race, gender and class.
2   Bilingualism is a positive asset, an important resource that nursery staff should recognise, value and build on in the classroom.
3   It is essential for nursery staff to create an environment where children's diverse cultural experiences are recognised and shared in a positive way.
4   Parents have a vital role to play in their children's education, both at home and at school. Their understanding of issues such as bilingualism, cultural diversity and racism can help to broaden the experience of everyone in the nursery.
5   The learning of English as a second language can be supported by:

   • bilingual children working and learning with their English-speaking peers
   • providing additional visual support
   • providing opportunities for rehearsal/repetition of natural language patterns
   • encouraging continued development of the home language
   • creating opportunities for informal interaction between adults and children and making maximum use of any opportunities that arise
   • creating opportunities in which spoken English is not a requirement for participation in an activity.

6   Children should not be withdrawn from the usual nursery activities for ESL work as this can:

   • deprive the children of a familiar supportive learning context where there are natural models of English
   • create divisions and resentment between children and pass on negative messages about the place of bilingualism in this society.

7   The cognitive development and linguistic development of children are closely linked and this needs to be considered when organising resources and activities both in children's home language(s) and in English.

References

Finkelstein, L (1990) 'Some children in my nursery don't speak English', *Primary Teaching Studies* 5(2): February.

In April 2008, Birgit wrote almost as much again, detailing the new things she was finding working with a larger team and meeting the needs of babies, toddlers and children. Sadly there is no room in this book to include all that she said. She reminds us of many things which seem to have become lost over the years – the fact that bilingual children need to be with both bilingual and monolingual learners in order to learn from and teach one another. In the next chapter, we see clearly just what very young children, who have learned more than one language, know about these languages and about language itself. The evidence of their metalinguistic awareness shines through their efforts to teach one another about their home languages.

Chapter 11

Learning about writing through bilingual peer teaching

Charmian Kenner

Charmian Kenner is a Lecturer in Educational Studies at Goldsmiths, University of London. She is the author of many books and papers.

Introduction

Peer teaching is one way of tapping into children's hidden bilingual resources, thus generating confidence and self-esteem. Even very young children can effectively teach others. A research project investigating children's understanding of different writing systems (Chinese, Arabic and Spanish) involved London 6-year-olds teaching their primary school classmates how to write in one of these languages (Kenner 2004). Selina and Ming were learning Chinese every weekend at a Saturday school run by the Chinese community. Tala and Yazan attended an Arabic school, while Sadhana and Brian studied at a Spanish school, also every Saturday. All the children's parents were keen for them to maintain the language of their family heritage, while also learning English at primary school. Each child enjoyed showing their peers how to write in Chinese, Arabic or Spanish. The 'pupils' responded well to their young teachers and quickly began to learn features of the new writing system. The primary school teachers involved were impressed by the bilingual children's knowledge. Relationships began to change, between these six children and their primary school classmates, and between the children and their teachers. In this chapter, I give examples of children learning through peer teaching, and suggest how similar activities could be incorporated into early years settings.

Young children from bilingual backgrounds already know a good deal about how language works. This knowledge can be used to build further learning, both for themselves and for their peers in early years settings. Yet when children are new to an educational setting that operates in English, they may at first seem less knowledgeable than others. They may be shy and rely on their English-speaking classmates for support.

Developing skills for writing: visual discrimination

When children begin to learn to write, in English or any other language, they need to pay careful attention to how one symbol looks different from another. Children learning Chinese have a head start in developing visual discrimination skills, and they can encourage their English school classmates to look closely at writing as well.

Each Chinese character is built up from a pattern of strokes, which children have to learn to recognise. A small difference in the stroke pattern can make the character look like another one with a different meaning. Children must notice how long each stroke is, what angle it is placed at, and whether it is straight or curved.

Selina, Ming and their classmates at the Chinese school were helped by their teachers, who would write a character on the board and ask children to spot the mistake. Children would point out that a stroke was 'too straight' (when it should be curved) or 'too far away' (when strokes should be placed closer together). They also had to write the strokes very precisely, and practise them many times, developing good pen control even at the age of 6 years. They sharpened their pencils often and tried to write their characters as elegantly as possible, because they knew Chinese writing should look beautiful. They often compared their efforts to those of their friends and decided whose writing was best.

One day Ming taught his Year 1 primary school class how to write in Chinese. Each child used a small whiteboard, as they often did for literacy lessons in English. Following Ming's example, they tried to copy the character for 'ten', which looks like a plus sign in English. Ming inspected the results and gave his opinion, saying for example 'it looks neat' or 'it's wonky and it's not straight'. Children began to realise that Chinese was not as easy as they had thought. They made greater efforts to get their lines straighter and the right length.

When Selina taught her friend Ruby on a one-to-one basis, she began by demonstrating an eight-step sequence of strokes for the character meaning 'tomorrow'. Ruby was keen to learn, but found the task a challenge. Selina checked her pupil's work and found it fell below her high standards. To Ruby's dismay, she rubbed out the entire column and showed her the sequence again. Ruby continued to have difficulties, so Selina adapted her teaching. She told her friend 'Pretend you're in Year 1 in Chinese school ... you can do easy ones' and gave Ruby a character with fewer strokes. Ruby started to look closely at her writing and make comparisons with Selina's example. She noticed when her strokes were not correct, making comments such as 'That bit was too long'. Gradually, Ruby improved the details of her strokes. She was proud of her Chinese writing and took it home to practise.

These examples show how children take their friends seriously as peer teachers, paying attention to their instructions. They start to work out what is important in the new writing system and change their own writing in order to receive positive feedback. Through trying to write Chinese, children can learn new skills in pen control and visual discrimination, which are also helpful for their writing in English.

Figure 11.1 Selina's Chinese writing: learning the stroke sequence to build up a character (right hand column) and practising the whole character many times

Directionality

Another skill for early literacy is working out in which direction writing goes. When children are learning both Arabic and English, they have to concentrate hard on this because the two scripts are produced in different directions. At the Arabic school attended by Yazan and Tala, teachers helped their pupils by constantly reminding them: 'Arabic – right to left; English – left to right'. The children then helped their classmates in English school to think about directionality. In a peer teaching session, Yazan showed how Arabic and English books went in different directions. He pointed to the front cover of his Arabic school textbook and stated 'Not the end'. Turning to the back cover, he emphasised 'This is the end'. And to make sure his audience was completely clear about the matter, he pointed to the front cover again and said 'This is the first'.

Tala required her classmates to focus on directionality of lines on the page. When she was teaching them to write the Arabic word '*mama*' ('mum'), they produced symbols which looked like hers but written from left to right. Tala told them 'No, that's wrong … we don't start from there, we start from here!', pointing to the right-hand rather than the left-hand side of the page. She put an arrow on the right-hand side of the paper to act as a reminder, just as her teacher sometimes did at Arabic school.

Young children tend to experiment with directionality in writing, as they decide which way is correct for particular letters, the line and the page. Sometimes it is thought that learning Arabic and English, or Urdu and English, at the same time would confuse children as they are trying to sort these issues out. Instead it seems to focus their attention on directionality. When I asked Tala to tell her primary school class the most important thing to remember about Arabic, she said 'Start the other way'.

Yazan showed he was thinking about directionality when doing a writing task in English in primary school. He asked me 'Which side shall we start? I think this side', pointing to the right-hand side of the page. Although he was wrong in this case, he was obviously thinking about the matter and knew there were two alternatives. Later, I saw Yazan correct himself at Arabic school, when he started to write an arithmetical sum in Arabic from left to right. He said, 'Oops, I did it wrong way', and rubbed it out, starting again from the right-hand corner of the page.

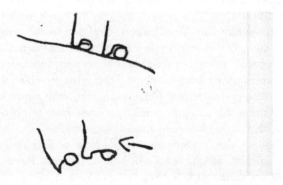

Figure 11.2 Arrow used by Tala to remind her classmates to start on the right when writing in Arabic

Comparing two writing systems can help children figure out the differences and understand better how each one works. Through peer teaching, children can discuss differences between writing systems with each other. As they think things over together, they clarify their ideas.

Understanding sound–symbol connections

When a language has the same script as English, children can compare how letters are linked with sounds. Does a letter that looks the same, sound the same? In Spanish, pronunciation always follows clear rules, which makes learning more straightforward than in English. Many consonants are pronounced as in English, but the vowels differ more, especially the letter 'i', which sounds like the letter-name 'E' in English. Children learning both English and Spanish have to work out the differences and remember to pay particular attention to such letters.

Teachers at Spanish school helped Brian, Sadhana and their other pupils with this task. They highlighted the Spanish 'i' by giving it a special name, so that children did not think of the English letter-name 'E' and write the letter 'e' instead. If Brian's teacher saw children writing '*pela*' instead of '*pila*', for example, she would remind them about '*la 'i' con sombrerito*' (the 'i' with the little hat, the 'hat' being the dot that would help them remember which letter they needed). Parents teaching their children at home had a similar approach. Sadhana's mother talked about '*la 'i' con palito y bolita*' (the 'i' with the little stick and the little ball).

Sadhana and Brian showed they were thinking about the difference between the Spanish 'i' and the English 'E'. When Sadhana was putting English alphabet letters in order, she asked her mother to pass 'E' and her mother gave her the letter 'i'. Sadhana said 'No!' and started singing the English primary school song beginning 'ABCDEFG' to point out to her mother that she wanted the English alphabet letter, not the Spanish one. One evening at home, Brian's grandmother reminded him to change 'e' to 'i' when he was writing a word in Spanish. Next day, Brian was teaching his friend Charlie at primary school. Charlie asked him why he had pointed to the letter 'i' and called it 'E', and Brian announced confidently: 'Because it's Spanish – it's different!'

Peer teaching can draw children's attention to different ways of pronouncing the same letter. For example, when Brian was teaching Jack how to write in Spanish, Jack enjoyed finding out about the different pronunciation of the letter 'i'. The two boys were making word searches for their class, in which the task was to find Spanish words in a grid of letters. Jack commented with amusement that if his classmates found the word '*mi*', they would not know how to pronounce it (they would not realise that it sounds like the English word 'me').

Children learning Spanish find out how vowels are linked with consonants to form syllables, which can then be built into words. For example, the consonant 'm' can be combined with 'a' to make 'ma', leading to the word '*mamá*' ('mum'). Brian had a Spanish textbook from Colombia, which he used at home with his mother and brother, showing a picture of a mother holding a child alongside the word '*mamá*'.

Brian

mi mama me ama

Figure 11.3 Spanish syllables: 'mi mamá me ama'

Below the picture were the syllables which could be formed from 'm' with each vowel: 'ma', 'me', 'mi', 'mo' and 'mu'. Next came the sentence 'mi mamá me ama' (my mum loves me).

In Spanish class, Brian and his classmates practised saying the syllables 'ma', 'me', 'mi', 'mo', and 'mu' many times. They often heard their teacher explaining in Spanish the principle of joining 'm' and 'a' to make 'ma'. She told them that letters without a vowel attached did not have a sound of their own. Brian then explained this principle to his English primary school class. He showed them the page about '*mamá*' in his Spanish book and told them 'The M on her own doesn't say anything – just 'mmm' – you have to put it together'. He pointed to the syllable 'ma' and said 'That's formed with the 'a' – with 'a' it makes 'ma'. Although many English words cannot be split so neatly into syllables, the idea of putting letters together to make particular sounds is also useful to children learning to read and write in English. Looking at the way Spanish works can make this idea clearer.

Setting up peer teaching

If you would like to set up peer teaching sessions in an early years setting, talk to children and their families to find out what languages are being taught at home. Are children learning at after-school or weekend classes too? Invite children to bring materials from home or community language class to your setting. Suggest they could teach a classmate, or a small group. Explain that their 'pupils' will be completely new to the writing system and will need plenty of help. The teaching process could be modelled by asking a confident bilingual child to demonstrate an aspect of writing to the whole class with the support of the class teacher. If the class has any difficulty following what to do, the teacher can ask questions and encourage the bilingual child to explain, to write more slowly or to demonstrate just one symbol at a time.

At first, families may be hesitant about offering materials, because they are not sure how their languages will be received. You can show your interest by bringing in newspapers or other items in different languages and asking if they have anything similar at home. If children are shy about being the teacher, you can invite parents and grandparents to come and be the first teachers, showing children how to write in their language. Ideally, this would be part of a range of activities that create a multilingual literacy environment in your setting – you will find many further ideas in the book *Home Pages* (Kenner 2000).

Children gain confidence when they and their parents or grandparents become the experts in their early years setting. By bringing in their knowledge of other writing systems and making comparisons with English, they can clarify their own ideas as they teach. Together with enhanced self-esteem, this supports their literacy development in both languages. Meanwhile, peer teaching offers a boost for all children's learning as they find out more about how writing works.

References

Kenner, C. (2000) *Home Pages: Literacy Links for Bilingual Children*, Stoke-on-Trent: Trentham Books.

Kenner, C. (2004) *Becoming Biliterate: Young Children Learning Different Writing Systems*, Stoke-on-Trent: Trentham Books.

This is a remarkable piece of research and brings together some of the themes of this book: what we can learn from watching and listening to children as they explore their own concerns; how remarkable young children are in making sense of all aspect of their world; and how social learning is. The next piece has been written by one of Kenner's students and refers to a small piece of research she carried out.

Chapter 12

How can bilingual children be supported in negotiating home and school environments in their early years?

Jacintha Moore

Jacintha Moore, a student of Charmian Kenner, carried out an investigation in an early years setting to gain a better understanding of how the relationship between the home and school environments works in the multicultural society in which education takes place today. The key questions considered were:

1 Is the importance of the link between home and school for bilingual children recognised?
2 Does the curriculum provide support for bilingual children in the early years in practice?
3 What are the ways in which the gaps between home and school environments can be bridged?

This piece is an extract from her work.

A number of education policies and resources to provide support for bilingual children have been put in place by successive UK governments. Currently, the suggested advice for early years on the inclusion of bilingual children requires early year's practitioners to: 'Find out about the child's ethnic, faith and cultural heritage and home experiences, so that familiar experiences and interests can be used as starting points for learning and teaching' (Qualifications and Curriculum Authority, QCA 2000: 12).

In our research we found tht:

- The attitudes of teaching staff were very contradictory. One said that 'Children are sort of allowed to speak their own languages in the classroom, but we always make a point of replying in English'. Another, that 'We do make a point of including other languages as we do value them. But we believe that English is the common language for survival and eventually children will pick up that their language is not for school and adapt their language use so they can fit in here'.
- There was a lack of understanding of what EAL actually means among practitioners. In this setting 'The policy is that everybody should be teaching EAL and

be aware of what that entails' was understood to mean, 'The current policy in relation to bilingualism is to support the children in order to communicate with them but we do not teach English as an additional language, but wait for them to learn the language by observing other children and staff in the setting and by the end of the term the children tend to be speaking English'.

- Resources need to be available to meet the needs of bilingual children. In this setting, resources were not extensive nor targeted specifically for bilingual children's use. While dual language books, scripts and artefacts were on display they were never observed as being used in teaching and seemed to be more for show than to provide support for bilingual children. When asked about this, a teacher explained, 'We have a few resources but they are not really used as we are too busy and don't have the time'. It is important that any resources available to support bilingual children are used properly.

- Developing good relationships with parents recognises their involvement in the education of bilingual children, both inside and outside of the home. There was a high degree of engagement with parents at the setting as it was recognised as important. 'As part of the admissions process, parents come in and fill in a form to register their interest. They are invited in for an open interview and the entry form is filled in together. A home visit to get to know the child and their home environment then takes place. Once a child starts at the setting there is a daily opportunity for parents to discuss issues with staff and information is made available on notice boards, in English'. From a bilingual perspective the main problem is that support and communication was mainly provided in English, especially newsletters, notices and other literature. Attempts have been made to engage with the parents by inviting them to be more involved in classroom activities. These are good ways to develop on-going relationships with parents which is key to understanding the link between home and school.

- It is important to be aware of and to have a view about how the gap between home and school could be bridged. In this setting, while it was acknowledged that there is a gap between these two environments and that policies in place could help with this, 'Think that the new Early Years Foundation Stage Curriculum will help to bridge the gap between home and school as it will be focused on supporting children from 0–5 years and providing a curriculum for them and therefore will be more holistic and will have to incorporate both home and school influences'. Despite this acknowledgement, there was no awareness that this was actually being played out and exacerbated as a direct result of practices being followed at this setting. These inconsistencies between policy and practice directly affected the manner of support being given to the bilingual child observed, who was left to 'sink or swim'.

In conclusion, research in this early years setting identified that there is a gap between home and school environments that bilingual children need to be supported in negotiating. Integrated home-school solutions could combine education policy and the research and understanding that experts have in this field, drawing on examples of good practice to show how this could be done. This would result in the influences of the home environment on bilingual children being better understood in the school environment, and in partnership with parents and children these could be integrated to ensure that all bilingual children receive equal support.

In the two chapters that follow, you can find a piece of action research by another of Kenner's students, and then a booklet for parents of children at a dream school designed by Cheryl Berbank who was a student at the University of East London. Part of the brief involved her in reflecting on what has been learned from research in a way that would be meaningful to parents.

Chapter 13

Storysacks
A piece of action research

Helen Gallagher

Helen Gallagher was doing a piece of action research as the culmination to her studies for an MA in Education at Goldsmiths College, University of London. The project involved working with Somali families and adapting 'storysacks' to make them more culturally relevant to this particular group. The study draws on participant observation, interviewing and audiotaping for its data and describes how storysacks can contribute to children's multi-modal development. The thinking behind it attempted to use what she calls 'Early Years pedagogy' but she tried to make it more culturally responsive to the families involved. The study concluded that there is a need to adapt approaches and resources in the early years if emergent bilinguals are to learn a new language and access a new culture with confidence and success. The study investigated play and early literacy as social and cultural practices that are co-constructed with others through joint involvement episodes. It argues in favour of family involvement in children's literacy development and finds evidence of 'synergy' between family members as well as a 'syncretic' combining of multiple influences. Overall, the findings suggest that children have a range of interests and a wealth of knowledge that are culturally related and that these areas of a child's development should be something early years professionals aim to actively discover, support and promote. This is a long and complex piece of work and we include here some extracts. Helen starts her piece by defining some terms:

- A *storysack* is a cloth drawstring bag containing a child's picture storybook and a selection of toys and props allowing the user to 'act out' the story. It may also include a non-fiction book and/or activity to complement the story. Neil Griffiths was responsible for creating the storysacks. He was a headteacher in Swindon and now directs the National Support Project for storysacks on behalf of the Basic Skills Agency.
- Tapes and/or adult helpers may be used and this allows stories to be read in different languages. The emphasis is thus on a *shared* experience of reading enabling a *two-way* process and offering many possibilities for learning and play.
- By offering this type of resource, it can be argued that certain assumptions have been made regarding narrative and active involvement in play. I will argue that although universal, these areas are culturally influenced and so the *experience* of

the bilingual child must also be engaged in order to maximise the learning potential of these resources.

- In order to address some of these assumptions, making storysacks *with* rather than *for* bilingual families became my main priority. The need for cultural sensitivity and paying special attention to the needs of bilingual learners is at the heart of this piece of research.

The setting

Most of the research took place in a playgroup set up to support a Somali Women's Group. While mothers were involved in keep-fit, a sewing group, English lessons and other activities the children were cared for by other parents, friends, relatives (usually grandmothers) and staff funded by SureStart, a government initiative that aims to help children, parents and communities by addressing health, education and employment needs. This particular part of South East London is included in the SureStart programme due to the amount of poverty and unemployment in the area. The aim was to find ways of supporting the children with the help of their families.

Action research

I began by visiting the group, observing children at play and informally interviewing parents. Parents discussed their children's interests and also their abilities in different languages. Most children heard Somali spoken at home so I decided to start with a dual language book written in Somali and English. One parent interview revealed that her son had a great interest in animals and could name many in his three languages (English, Somali and Arabic). This interest had been sparked by his grandmother's stories of living on a farm in Somalia. Halima enjoyed unloading her mother's scarf drawer at home and using the scarves for covering and wrapping things as well as for dressing up. Three of the children were very young, so using soft toys was a consideration. A number of parents had referred to the influence of grandparents on both them and their children. Some were close by and actively involved and others were in Africa and sadly missed. There was also a desire to help children feel comfortable with their abilities rather than embarrassed to speak in languages other than English. This issue came up frequently, especially in relation to older siblings who would not speak home languages outside. Based on this data, the first storysack session was planned.

The first session

Walking Through the Jungle/Dhex Lugee Kaynta by Debi Harter (2004) has a simple, rhythmic and repetitive text and is beautifully illustrated. The child in the story travels around the world on an imaginary adventure discovering different animals in different locations. Although the locations might not be familiar to the children they are varied and are not culturally specific. There is plenty of opportunity for talk and play and for children to bring their own ideas and interests to the sharing of this book.

The storysack contained the various soft-toy animals, a doll with brown skin to represent both the child in the story and the children in the group and a selection of scarves representing the different photographic landscapes in the book. Scarves are important culturally as most of the women in the group wore scarves to cover their heads.

Hussein's mother agreed to read the book in Somali and English.

The children's responses

Hussein (age 3½)

Hussein responded positively to his mother's involvement and seemed much more vocal and animated than I had seen him previously. He repeated animal names in English and smiled at his mother as she read in Somali. She, in turn, directed certain questions towards him and received much positive feedback on her reading of the story. Kenner (2000) emphasises the effects of parental involvement for bilingual children who may be aware that society accords greater power to the English language. They therefore need opportunities to see their home languages valued more often. Hussein also named certain animals for my benefit as he manoeuvred the toys. With his mother's encouragement he wiggled the snake and taught me 'mas' and then 'libaax' for lion. We then said the words in keeping with the nature of the animal, 'masssss' and 'libaax' with a roar. I realised that the use of toys to emphasise certain features in a dramatic way may help towards learning vocabulary in a new language. As Pahl (1999) suggests, children need opportunities to go from two to three-dimensions in their learning. Integrating movement, a three-dimensional object and a label helped me to remember certain words more easily and similarly would assist emergent bilinguals with learning a new language.

Ahmed (age 2)

Ahmed's mother translated the animal names into Arabic as this was his stronger language at that time. He was a little worried about the snake and the wolf toys but really liked playing with the lion. Mum said lions are his favourite animals. The soft toys were especially appealing to the younger children particularly if, as in this case, they could also produce sound effects. The lion roars and says, 'I am a lion, the king of the jungle and everybody listens when I roar, I'm your friend ROAR!!' These 'chunks' of language (Hatch 1974), often experienced through play and song or rhyme, can be important in learning whole expressions in appropriate contexts. The words do not need to be fully understood, as it is the context that becomes familiar and therefore assists with language learning. Mostly Ahmed's interaction was with his mother as may be expected bearing in mind his age. The security of this relationship helped Ahmed move outwards and he was engaging with the toys and watching other children's reactions.

Yusuf (age 3¾)

Yusuf seemed the most keen to actually act out the story using all the props. He asked many times, 'What's this?' and was looking to acquire labels for everything, displaying a strong *lexical* understanding, often the case with 'emergent bilinguals' (Gregory 1996). He hid the animals in the scarves and quickly understood the *semantic* aspect of the story and the build up to a new animal each time, which took the form of a repeated refrain: 'Walking through the jungle. What do I see?'

This chanting rhythm was very well supported by the mothers and Yusuf picked it up quickly. He shouted out names in English and again, but more quietly, in Somali. This could have been shyness about speaking in Somali or perhaps, as Ahlam (Ibrahim's mother) had observed, he was aware of different cultural expectations with regard to Western school 'storytime' behaviour.

At the end of the book, there is a picture of the animals sleeping and Yusuf was determined to balance them on top of each other in exactly the same way. One of his persistent interests was ordering and sequencing.

Ngozi (age 1 year and 11 months)

Ngozi was the youngest in the group. She was very interested in what was inside the bag and the element of surprise often seemed an appealing feature of the storysacks for her. She was keen to look at the animals but seemed even more interested in the scarves for dressing up and covering her face to play peekaboo. On another occasion, she used a scarf to tie a baby to her back and was often to be seen transporting dolls in pushchairs using the scarves as covers (two culturally different ways of transporting babies). Other younger children also joined in with the peekaboo game and so were stimulated by her ideas.

Summary of the action research issues

A number of issues were highlighted through observation and analysis. Based on the younger children's creative use of scarves a consideration of resources that are more open-ended in relation to play seemed appropriate. A scarf, as observed, can be used to make meaning in many different ways.

Also finding ways to incorporate different scripts in the storysacks was an important issue for parents. Arabic was being taught to most of the children and they attend more formal instruction around age 5 years. Yusuf was already attending Arabic lessons as well as a French club organised by SureStart.

Parents often discussed similarities and differences in languages among themselves and referred to their own strengths and weaknesses. By cutting out pictures of the various animals from card it was possible to write the names in different scripts on the back. When parents helped with this, it also led to interesting 'joint involvement episodes'. Halima made a snake with her mother and while writing on the back was asked whether it was Somali or English. 'I write everything' was the reply.

Kress (1997) emphasises the power of cutting out. When drawings can be moved around in space, they are brought into the world of physical objects here and now, then re-animated in the imaginative effort of the child. In this example, the *text* could also be lifted from the page and moved around in order to give more emphasis to the different scripts being used. The link between the object and the label may be seen more clearly.

Using chunks of language also became a consideration, as songs and rhymes were particularly appealing to the youngest children, along with the soft toys.

A joint involvement episode

The question that is addressed here is whether storysacks can be seen to promote joint involvement episodes that take place within the security of the caregiver relationship and therefore assist children's language development and learning?

Having read the story, *Walking Through the Jungle,* I decided to make some of the animals from card in order to stick labels written in different languages on the back. At the same time children made snakes by cutting card into spiral shapes and decorating them. This gave opportunities to cut out and move from two- to three-dimensional representation with adults helping their children, paying joint attention and acting together on an object (Schaffer 1992). Adults were also writing on labels in different languages, so that these could be stuck on to the animal shapes.

Here is what happened when Halima and her mother were making a snake together:

H: See green, yellow [she makes spots on the snake].
M: [Speaks first in Somali] cagaar (green), huruudi (yellow). That's nice Halima.
H: I do like this [continues making spots].
M: One, two, three, four, five [uses English first] kow, labo, sadax [stops as Halima counts].
H: One … two … three … five … six [misses out four so mum reminds her].
M: Can you make these lines? [Mum makes some lines in a row. We talked about the pink and green stripes on the snake in the story earlier].
H: I do it [she tries to copy but it takes a bit more help from Mum].

Then Halima continues with very careful stripes all around the snake.

They continue to talk in Somali. Halima notices some scissors and begins cutting small pieces of paper. She then glues them onto her snake with a glue stick. She then 'writes' (squiggles) on each tiny piece. This is her way of copying the adults around who have been sticking words onto the card animals.

M: I didn't know you could do that Halima, that's good, that's very nice.
H: I can do it see [continues to write more]. I write it like this [points to the labels].
M: Oh, you are writing like me? Somali or English?
H: I write everything.

Here we can see early literacy attempts fully supported by these parents, giving children the kind of encouragement that assists their development as communicators. Halima's mother was very pleased and proud of Halima's skills using scissors and glue. Her interest and support highlighted the concept of 'scaffolding' and the importance of sensitive others (Bruner 1996).

Halima was being supported in two languages and inducted into her own culture through story and language. There were also opportunities for adult creativity and for Halima to bring her own creative ideas to her making of the snake. Gregory (1996) emphasises the mutual benefits for children and mothers as they make resources in home languages. Halima has merged storytelling experience with written activity encouraged by watching adults. The resources used can be seen as *cultural tools* assisting as well as shaping shared understandings in a particular context. Halima is helped to develop her own intentions and capabilities through the 'intersubjective' relationship with her mother who acts *as if* she already has these intentions (Anning and Edwards 1999). She has developed confidence and self-esteem as can be seen from her final comment to her mother, '*I write everything!*'

Grandparent and child

The idea of the storysack as a cultural tool for developing shared understandings is particularly useful when considering the wider family network. These resources are aimed specifically at families and are made for use in the home by all members, young and old.

After reading the story, *Splash* (McDonnell 2004) the children were playing with the various animals and a long silky scarf representing the water. Yusuf's grandmother entered and after greeting the adults she joined the children in her characteristically lively way (she was a great favourite among the children).

G: Give me salaam! [She indicates that the children all 'give her five' on her hand and goes round the whole group in this way. The children are all amused and happy to see her. Different cultural forms of address are creatively melded here by Yusuf's grandmother].

Yusuf [excitedly]: Rhino look he splash in the water.

Grandmother engages in play with the children speaking in Somali. Unfortunately, I can't understand so I ask Faridha (Yusuf's mother) to help. Apparently, Yusuf had previously heard his grandmother tell a story about the rhino's horn (this is why he has drawn her attention to the toy rhino). Faridha says the word in Somali and asks me for the English, horn or tusk maybe?

Yusuf tunes into this conversation smiling at his mother and telling her the Arabic word. Faridha repeats this slowly helping him with the precise pronunciation as on numerous other occasions. The sounds in Arabic are very precise and need close attention. As noted by Jessel et al. (2004) pronunciation is seen as very important in learning Arabic in contrast to Western educational practice that gives higher priority to meaning. As they develop 'metalinguistic' awareness, children use cues they have acquired from various sources and teachers will need to be aware of the possibility of different teaching strategies that may have influenced their development (Gregory et al. 2004).

Grandma then asks the children (in Somali) about the 'Splash' (McDonnell 2004) story. She leafs through the book pointing out things in the pictures.

Y: Horn, it cut you [he play fights with the rhino and the elephant. The two boys Yusuf and Hussein squabble over the animals and pull the piece of fabric].

G: [Speaks Somali and stops the fighting. Apparently she asks if they think they are rhinos! She has authority and humour in this situation and both boys stop. She then diverts their attention and asks about the elephant's tusks and trunk].

Y: Elephant, maroodi ... [speaks Somali and puts it in the water] Splash, splash, he drink it the water with his horn [points to trunk] trunk, this trunk [self corrects] You say it.

G: Ah, trunk [laughs].

Grandmother later takes the book written in Somali and English to Hussein's mother who reads Somali.

Somali has only been a written language since 1972 and Yusuf's grandmother does not read the language but is obviously interested to hear parts of the story read.

It was interesting to see Yusuf assuming the role of expert and trying to give his grandmother the English labels. This had also happened in a different language on a previous occasion when a carer had needed an Arabic word (she didn't understand the Somali) and Yusuf had shouted out the translation. He already 'code switches' competently in order to converse with different people and here young and old can be seen learning from each other and pushing each other on. The rhino story told in Somali was again an example of guided participation and was prompted through the use of the storysack. The picture book may not be a familiar 'tool' for the grandmother but elements of the provision did give her the opportunity to share parts of her cultural heritage with the children. Hence, different kinds of knowledge were exchanged. Grandparents often have more time and within this community they are regularly involved in looking after their grandchildren. As indicated by Jessel et al. (2004) the learning taking place here is a two way process. If storysacks of this kind go into homes, it is hoped that they will offer opportunities for 'synergy' of this kind.

References

Anning, A. and Edwards, A. (1999) *Promoting Children's Learning from Birth to Five*, Buckingham: Open University Press.

Bruner, J.S. (1996) *The Culture of Education*, Cambridge, MA: Harvard University Press.

Gregory, E. (1996) *Making Sense of a New World: Learning to Read in a Second Language*, London: Paul Chapman.

Harter, D. (2004) *Dhex Lugee Kaynta/Walking Through the Jungle*, Bath: Barefoot Books.

Hatch, E. (1974) 'Research on reading in a second language', *Journal of Reading Behaviour* 6: 53–61.

Jessel, J., Gregory, E., Arju, T., Kenner, C. and Ruby, M. (2004) 'Children and their grand-parents at home: a mutually supportive context for learning and linguistic development' *English Quarterly*, December.

Kenner, C. (2000) *Home Pages: Literacy Links for Bilingual Children*, Stoke-on-Trent: Trentham Books.

Kress, G. (1997) *Before Writing: Rethinking Paths to Literacy*, London: Routledge.

McDonnell, F. (2004) *Splash!* London: Mantra Lingua.

Pahl, K. (1999) *Transformations: Meaning Making in Nursery Education*, Stoke-on-Trent: Trentham Books.

Schaffer, H.R. (1992) 'Joint involvement episodes as contexts for cognitive development', in H. McGurk (ed.) *Childhood and Social Development: Contemporary Perspectives*, Hove: Lawrence Erlbaum.

There are some delightful things in this piece which illustrate many of the issues being addressed in this book.

Chapter 14

My dream school

A booklet for parents

Cheryl Berbank

Welcome to ...

Welcome to our school!

There are over 400 children currently on the school roll. Over 30% of them are children who are learning English as an Additional Language (EAL). There are currently 38 languages, other than English, spoken in our school. We value and respect the diversity of the cultures and languages that your children bring to our school. We believe that a multicultural and multilingual environment enriches the lives of all children, from all backgrounds.

It is important that children feel proud of their linguistic skills and heritage. It is also important for them to learn English in order to gain an education in the UK. Therefore, we believe that our commitment to your children's learning and development should promote their learning in its widest sense: academic, personal and social. This booklet sets out to explain how we intend to achieve this.

We hope your child will learn a great deal while they are with us, that they will feel safe and secure and that they will discover the pleasure of learning.

Our Aims ...

In order to promote and support your children's learning and development, it is essential that their ethnic, cultural, religious and linguistic backgrounds are positively reflected throughout our school. Additionally, the Race Relations (Amendment) Act (2000) places a statutory duty on all schools to promote equality of opportunity and challenge prejudice and racism across all aspects of the school. This applies to the curriculum, resources, displays as well as attitudes and behaviour of the school community.

In order to support your children we aim to:

- Help EAL learners to develop their skills in speaking, listening, reading and writing.
- Encourage and further develop EAL learners' home language.
- Enable EAL learners to access all subjects covered by the National Curriculum through the medium of English.
- Support all children's self-esteem and confidence in their own ethnicity by positively promoting a multicultural society.
- Recognise and educate against prejudice and racism.

Personal and Social Development ...

A sense of belonging

Research has shown that children learn best when they feel safe, secure, valued and are able to develop a sense of belonging.

Assemblies

We consider school assemblies to be an important aspect of school life. They are a daily event whereby the school may celebrate a variety of multicultural festivals, religious occasions or personal achievement. Assemblies may also afford EAL learners opportunities to hear English spoken – which research has shown to be an important part of their second language development. Assemblies enable us to recognise and support two important areas of your children's lives.

Spiritual and traditional occasions

As a multicultural community we recognise and celebrate a range of special occasions: Diwali, Hanukah, Chinese New Year or Christmas, as examples. We encourage children to share with the school, the spiritual or traditional meanings of these occasions. Children participate in these assemblies by reading a written account of how their families celebrate, a religious story explaining the meaning of the occasion, drama, traditional song or dance to name a few. In doing so, we feel that children's individual and cultural identities are reinforced and positively promoted. It also encourages all children, through a deeper understanding, to appreciate the commonalities as well as respect the differences within our school community.

Personal achievements

Assemblies also provide opportunities to celebrate and share the children's achievements: academic and non-academic; in and out of school. School certificates for a variety of reasons, including academic progression for example, are presented to the children. Additionally, some children participate in a variety of clubs outside school: sport, drama, music, etc., and we acknowledge their achievements in these clubs. Children's self-esteem may be nurtured and their achievements celebrated.

Social activities

There are a variety of activities throughout the school day for your children to socialise with their peers in a less structured environment. Playtime, lunch breaks and school clubs are typical examples. We consider these activities to be as important as your children's academic learning. They provide opportunities for children to integrate into the school community, develop friendships and support their language acquisition, in both their home language and English.

Academic Achievement ...

Your child's learning

The Swann Report (1985) had a significant impact on the structure of our education system – particularly for EAL learners. The report recommended that EAL learners should be taught alongside their peers in the mainstream classroom.

As a result, the Education Reform Act (1988) was passed and the National Curriculum (NC) established. The NC provides a framework for teaching a variety of subjects. In particular, the Literacy Hour assists children in developing their speaking, listening, reading and writing skills. These are essential skills that aid achievement across the school curriculum. The Literacy Hour provides a framework that develops children's literacy skills using a range of texts: fiction, non-fiction and poetry, from a diversity of writers and cultures.

In order to gain an education in the UK, it is important for EAL learners to be literate in English. However, research has shown that maintenance and development of an EAL learner's home language, is beneficial to their academic achievements. Therefore our commitment to your child's academic achievements requires balancing the continued development of home language while nurturing their English. We aim to support your child's learning and development in a variety of ways:

- Build on your child's previous experience, thus activating their prior knowledge
- Provide a variety of resources that reflect the cultural diversity within our school
- Where possible, to promote the use of their home language, through the support of Bilingual Assistants or peers who share the same language
- Provide opportunities to practise their speaking and listening skills through a range of teaching styles that include group/paired discussions with English-speaking peers
- Provide a range of materials to support the development of their reading and writing skills – dual language books, writing frames and visual support for subjects across the curriculum.

Part IV

Children as thinkers and problem-solvers

This is a section new for this edition of the book and it starts with a chapter about young children and numbers. The piece has been specially written for this book by Hilary Faust, an acknowledged expert in the field. The other contributions in this part will be familiar to those of you who read the first edition of this book. They are wonderful observation notes made by Maria Figuerido, Mary Smith and Sarah Cotter, all of whom were students on the Early Childhood Studies Scheme at the time and all of whom paid such respectful attention to the questions children ask and the theories they devise.

Chapter 15

Mathematical development in the Early Years Foundation Stage

Problem-solving, reasoning and numeracy

Hilary Faust

Hilary Faust has been involved in early years education and care for many years and has developed a reputation as an expert in early years mathematics. She is currently involved in working as a trainer and consultant. You will find her ideas about creating an enabling environment extremely helpful.

Babies' and children's mathematical development occurs as they seek patterns, make connections and recognise relationships through finding out about and working with numbers and counting, with sorting and matching and with shape, space and measures.

(Early Years Foundation Stage, EYFS)

This definition suggests that mathematics is to do with young children making sense of a complex world, and dealing with everyday experiences and problems, not just carrying out school or nursery tasks. We know that young children begin this process as new babies. For example, reaching out to grasp a finger involves developing spatial concepts; engaging in turn-taking interactions with a carer is the beginning of recognising and enacting a pattern. Distinguishing the mother's face from other faces involves recognising similarities and differences, an important aspect of maths – and it is well recorded that babies can recognise up to three items from birth (Karmiloff-Smith 1994).

So – maths comes into everything we do right from the start.

Tuning in to babies and children

For the early years practitioner, one of the most important skills is recognising the mathematical in what young children do as they play and explore. Being able to spot this allows us to support and extend this learning and development when appropriate.

Here's an observation of Amit (23 months)

Amit walks over to the home corner, chooses a basket and proceeds to fill it with anything he can lay his hands on. When it is nearly full he picks it up, registering the surprising change in weight, and carries it to the carpet where he unpacks it all with great satisfaction.

A practitioner who observes this might consider several mathematical possibilities:

- He's interested in a transporting schema, moving things from one place to another, and through that, learning about distance, position and space.
- All that filling and emptying means he is interested in an enclosure schema, and through that, learning about capacity, full and empty.
- He is learning about weight when he notices that the full bag feels different from the empty one.

It seems clear that young children's schematic learning is often very mathematical. Worthington and Carruthers (2003) have a fascinating and informative chapter in their book *Children's Mathematics*, where they see many schemas as helping children to grasp mathematical ideas intuitively, providing a 'thought footstool' for many more complicated mathematical ideas:

> Very early schemas can combine together, for example:
>
> - horizontal schema – carefully lining objects up horizontally
> - connecting schema – lining objects up, one touching the other
> - number schema – putting numbers to objects but not necessarily in the standard way.
> - children using numbers in their everyday talk.
>
> Eventually these schemas can work together to produce counting.
>
> (Worthington and Carruthers 2003: 37)

We can recognise a circularity/rotation schema in the 3-year-old who repeatedly traces the rim of the round water tray with a paint brush, spends ages stirring the papier mâché mixture, paints and draws circles, screws and unscrews round jar lids, rolls over and over down the grassy slope. Worthington and Carruthers discuss a similar schema explored by Zoe (4 years, 7 months):

> For over 2 terms everyone in the class knew she had a passion for spirals. She drew them, cut out spirals and talked about them endlessly. Outside she often walked in a spiral formation … saying 'I'm winding myself up', and then, reversing her direction, announced 'I'm unwinding myself' … One day her mother brought in some Greek cakes called 'baklavas' … Zoe proudly told her friend that 'they're spirals'.
>
> (Worthington and Carruthers 2003: 43)

They go on to describe the teachers' responses to Zoe, including mixing fruits and jam into yoghurt, providing pastry and dried fruit to roll up, introducing African snails with spiral shells, providing ropes and wools which led to creating mazes.

Having such a 'window' into Zoe's mind provides a wonderful opportunity for the practitioners to encourage mathematical concepts and language related to shape, space, position and direction through resources and activities, using her persistent concerns as a starting point for her and other children engaged in similar schemas.

Talking maths

What the practitioner says to the child is of course very important. Let us return to Amit and the basket: a practitioner might talk with him about what he is so intent on doing, perhaps commenting:

> 'You're filling the basket right up!'
> 'Oh, does it feel heavy now?'
> 'You've moved all these things a long way!'

Feeding in mathematical language like this gives the child words to think and communicate with. Open questions can be very useful, but it is important to not only ask questions. Reflecting back to the child what he is doing can often be a more effective interaction, sometimes, as with a good question, leading to the 'sustained shared thinking', which has been recognised as the essence of good teaching (EYFS: 9) Getting involved in the thinking process with the child in this way is the key to good practice.

We might also plan to support and extend an interest in transporting, which other children may well share. One setting decided to do this, and set out a blanket on the floor with baskets and bags of different shapes and sizes and a range of fruits and vegetables. Two children showed an immediate interest and proceeded to repeatedly fill up the bags and carried them around. After some time, one child became interested in sorting out the different sizes of potatoes. The practitioner chatted with the children about what they were doing, noticing what they seemed to be particularly concerned with, introducing mathematical language but being careful not to highjack the play by imposing her own agenda.

A baby sitter was playing with a little girl of two and a half. The child chose some plastic fruit segments which fitted together with Velcro, and the adult talked with her about them. 'You've got two pieces there haven't you? When you take them apart like that you've got two halves', and so on. Later that evening the two of them were lying on the child's bed, in a bid to get her to go to sleep. The adult said 'two sleepy girls', to which the child responded in a puzzled tone, 'but we're not cut in half!'

We can see how the child is using the mathematical language and thinking introduced casually before bed, to explore and extend her current understanding of 'two' and of 'halves', puzzling out why the adult used the word two in a different context. Even at such a young age, children's brains are working overtime to make sense of new information, so it is really important to give them the language to think with as well as concepts to think about, even if they cannot fully understand them yet.

An enabling physical environment

We can see from the previous examples that maths learning and teaching can take place anywhere, and are by no means restricted to the maths area or corner. The concept of a print-rich environment is familiar, but it is important also to think about a number-rich environment, where written numbers are displayed for real, meaningful purposes. With very young children, this will apply to a lesser extent, as they will not be developmentally ready to deal with symbols such as numerals, but including some in the environment will help to familiarise them.

In the home corner, providing items such as calendars and clocks, remote controls and mobile phones, numbers on the cooker, a microwave or washing machine, bathroom scales and a tape measure will all offer opportunities for children to notice numbers and engage with them in their play. Of course, this also applies to other imaginative role-play scenarios, where there is always scope for including numbers.

Providing a magnetic board is accepted as good practice for language and literacy development, but we can also focus on number in this way. When children are familiar with number rhymes like 'Five Green Speckled Frogs', it can be supportive to place magnetic frog cut-outs on the board. This allows children to revisit the experience of singing and acting out the number rhyme, to be in control and make sense of the language and concepts involved. It can be appropriate with older children to introduce number symbols as they act out a well known rhyme; the practitioner shows a card with 5 and changes the numbers until 0 represents no more frogs. Eventually the children can take it in turns to find the correct number card. To accompany this extension, magnetic numbers can appear with the frog cut outs.

There are many rhymes and books that help children to focus on numbers. Building on *Kipper's Toy Box* (Inkpen 1992) offers an opportunity to engage in simple addition and subtraction by providing a cardboard box, a supply of toys and a dice. Although magnetic pictures are supportive, young children learn most effectively through handling real objects, using their senses more fully. For example, providing small cats can encourage children to see how many cats they can fit in a box (capacity), inspired by the book *My Cat Likes to Hide in Boxes* (Eve Sutton 1973). The practitioner can introduce games involving working out how many cats are hiding if there are so many visible outside the box. This involves the children in valuable mental calculation.

When organising the environment, labelling containers with labels saying things like '5 scissors' or '6 pens' supports learning and makes tidy-up time an opportunity for counting and calculating how many items are missing.

The outside area should provide plenty of opportunities for maths. Here are some ideas:

- Marking out number tracks or hopscotch, permanently or with chalk
- Games with big dice, collecting bean bags, jumping on the number track
- Numbering the vehicles with accompanying numbered parking bays
- Making registration numbers for the vehicles

- Making bus stops with familiar bus numbers displayed
- Games like skittles, basketball or completing an obstacle course which involves scoring, counting and possibly addition
- Encouraging children to record their scores by providing plenty of clipboards, easels, white boards, post-its and chalks
- Treasure hunts, hiding and finding wooden or plastic numerals
- Making a role-play garage with numbered petrol pumps and prices
- Hiding 'treasure' in the sand pit and counting out how many shells, and so on.

Back inside, providing number lines, either fixed or moveable like a washing line with number cards pegged on, and other arrays of numbers such as 100 squares or number mats help children to develop a picture of what the number system looks like and how it works. Over time, children will begin to hold these images of numbers in their heads, and this will help them to calculate mentally, which is central to developing numeracy.

Organising found materials can involve children in sorting and classifying for a real purpose. Having all the lids, cylinders, cuboid boxes and so on in separate containers, will encourage parents who bring in bags of 'junk' to sort them with their child, using mathematical language and concepts as they do so.

As we know, there is more to maths than number (despite the new emphasis in the EYFS wording), so we need to provide interesting resources to encourage sorting and classification, learning about sequence and pattern, shape, space and measurement. We are often tempted by expensive items from catalogues, and while sometimes these can be of value, providing collections of real items, like shoes, socks, keys, buttons or brushes can often engage the children more successfully, as they are rich and interesting items relating to the real world, rather than a group of similar plastic objects. Think about how a collection of spoons can be very useful in engaging children. They might focus on the length of handles and size of the bowls or automatically sort them in different ways, by material, size or perhaps all those with holes in. They might order them according to size or shape. The spoons can spark off imaginative play, maybe pretending a giant would use the really huge spoon and finding other kitchen items large enough for a giant's kitchen.

Such collections are essentially mathematical because they all have a common feature and yet they differ, introducing the question of how items relate to each other; how are they the same and how are they different. Collections can be more abstract and challenging, such as things with holes in or in a spiral shape. It is good to have larger scale collections outside too, such as things that roll, lengths of different materials that can be joined together or a collection of plant pots.

Boxes are usually available for modelling or play and provide many opportunities for learning about shape, space and measurement as well as delighting the children who are into an enclosure and containing schema. Having huge boxes, indoors and out, can lead to all sorts of play and creativity, discussing position, shape, size as they clamber in and out or convert them for their own purposes, solving different problems as they do so.

Providing different sized dolls and different sized dolls' clothes inevitably leads to discussions of measurement and problem-solving. This can also be achieved when changing a child. Some practitioners make 'deliberate mistakes' by fetching the wrong sized socks which encourages discussion and problem-solving as together they search for the right size. This can be particularly effective with younger children.

The opportunities are endless, and practitioners can focus children's attention on the mathematical through what they provide. Linda Pound (1999) gives an example of this, describing a nursery team's planning to encourage the children to consider length.

> In the outside water area they added piping of all lengths – some very short, some very long. In the creative workshop area they added a large number of very short and very long cardboard tubes. Into the dressing up area were placed long pieces of ribbon and material. Long and short straws were placed on the milk table.
>
> (Pound 1999)

The pedagogical environment

As well as the physical environment, it is important to consider the pedagogical environment, or the ethos of the group or class. For instance, are children encouraged to make their own graphic representations, or are they expected to complete adult-created worksheets or written tasks? Worthington and Carruthers (2003) have encouraged practitioners to consider children's own mark-making as potentially mathematical and emphasise the importance of recognising and analysing such 'graphic representations'. They have researched the beneficial effect of this approach on children's mathematical development, discussing the similarity with literacy development, moving from individual, personal representations towards standard forms of maths recording.

This approach depends on providing a range of mark-making materials all around the setting, practitioners suggesting children put something on paper when appropriate and modelling standard forms in meaningful contexts when children are ready for this. So in nursery and reception classes, helping the milkman in a story who keeps getting deliveries wrong (Faust 2004) might involve the children and practitioner in writing down the number of bottles required.

It is also important for the practitioner to talk with children about their mark-making and how it represents their maths thinking. Worthington and Carruthers give the example of a child new to Reception who decided to draw a picture of her younger sister, also conveying that she was two and a half. She wrote a recognisable numeral for 2 and then solved the problem of representing a half by writing a mark that looked like half a 2. Such examples illustrate how creative maths can be, but it takes sensitivity, experience and some imagination to recognise what such children are attempting, and then talking with them about it.

The recent Williams Report, reviewing maths teaching in early years settings and primary schools (Williams 2008) has recommended that the DCSF commissions a set of materials on mathematical mark–making, thus acknowledging the central role this can play in young children's mathematical development. They quote a nursery headteacher who says of the early mark-making,

> We believe this is the very beginning of the process of children understanding the abstract symbolism of maths.
>
> (Williams 2008: 35)

Many practitioners and parents will recollect even 2-year-olds making meaningful marks. One child (2 years, 4 months) who spent a lot of time at his parent's office, spontaneously filled in a bank form, making numeral type marks in the columns provided.

Problem-solving

Another aspect in providing a positive ethos is encouraging risk taking and creativity, important parts of the problem–solving process which has now been acknowledged as central to maths development (EYFS).

We have seen several examples of young children solving problems, both posed by an adult as well as those initiated by the child. Of the latter, Linda Pound writes,

> Their enthusiasms provide the motivation to become not merely problem-solvers, but problem finders. Problem finding involves passionately wanting to know something. It provides children with a much greater drive than simply being presented with a problem to solve … Many of our problem-solving strategies arise out of a trial and error approach. We guess what will work based on what has worked elsewhere, try it out and then try something else if it doesn't do the trick.
>
> (*Nursery World* 2008)

Allowing children plenty of time to approach things in this way, and not rushing in to solve their problem, supports an enabling ethos. This might be a child trying to attach 'arms' to a robot, finding the right bricks to complete the mosque she has decided to build, finding enough cylindrical shaped objects to complete the perimeter she has started to surround the table top, mixing enough paint to cover a big box, turning it into a postbox, working out how many pieces of pizza he'll need for his party guests. Sometimes the problems children set themselves can be easily overlooked or dismissed, but in a positive environment, this is less likely.

In a useful book produced by 'The Early Childhood Mathematical Group' and BEAM (1997) they consider some things to say to children to encourage development in problem-solving.

'Why won't it fit?'
'What can you do?'

'What have you thought of so far?'
'What could you use to help you?'
'Have you seen something like this before?'

And of course, comments rather than just questions, for example:

'I wonder why it won't fit'
'I can see you're looking for all the cylindrical shapes'
'You're trying lots of different ways to attach the arms'
'Let me know if you'd like some help'

can be encouraging and helpful.

Active, play-based learning

We know that using their senses and moving freely are the natural ways for young children to learn. Anyone with experience of young children knows that sitting still is very difficult for many children, especially for boys. And we also know from research that children need to move. Linda Pound (1999) points out,

> It is physical movement which enables humans to develop complex thinking in both halves of their brain. As such it is vital to the education of young children.
>
> (Pound 1999: 30)

We clearly should not be seeing maths learning as something children get just from listening to adults on the carpet or sitting at tables doing worksheets. It is valuable to do short bursts of number rhymes, stories and games in groups, especially following a period of play and activity and depending on the age and stage of the children.

The EPPE research project has emphasised the importance of maintaining a good balance between adult and child directed learning and too much whole class work upsets the balance. The younger the child, the more he/she needs to direct his/her own learning, because it is much easier to follow a thought in your own head than somebody else's, especially if you can do this with some sensitive support.

Practitioners need to consider how best to incorporate maths into physically active experiences. Here is an example:

> Children in a nursery outside area became totally involved in a game which required them to throw a dice, collect the right number of beanbags, climb a short ladder and post them down the drain pipe attached to the fence. This led on to some children recording their scores in a variety of personal ways. When asked if they would like to put something on the paper to show how many they had got, some declined, some drew bean bags, some tallies, some attempted the number symbol.

This opportunity to record something meaningful to them in any way they chose involves real mathematical thinking, rather than simply copying a symbol.

Worthwhile, meaningful experiences

As well as observing, supporting and extending children's play and exploration, practitioners should introduce experiences based on their interests and needs. The more children can understand the purposes involved, the more effective the learning will be. 'Real life' activities, such as cooking, making ice lollies, wallpapering the home corner or making tablecloths for a party, have great potential for maths learning and teaching. Here is an example:

> A group of four 3-year-olds is making sandwiches for a teddy bears' picnic. They have been given sliced brown bread of two different sizes, cheese spread and bananas, as well as knives and plates. A practitioner is at the table, supporting the children, feeding in the relevant language and assisting where necessary.

Children are learning about the shape and size of the bread slices, counting slices, matching two slices of the same size, cutting the sandwiches into halves and quarters, the different shape of the sandwiches (squares or triangles). They might decide how much cheese or banana they need and how many sandwiches can fit on the plate, arranging banana slices or spreading the cheese to cover the bread.

With older children, you could add another filling and have white as well as brown bread to increase the possible combinations. There could be more focus on taking orders for preferred sandwiches, possibly using a graph or chart, introducing data handling and numbers.

Good early years practice often involves allowing children to revisit such an activity through play. In this case, it might involve providing knives and plates with assorted materials for fillings. Some settings allow children to repeat such real experience on a regular basis, for example, having a table constantly available with cheap sliced bread and spread. As we know, children often need to repeat activities many times, be it making a sandwich or filling a bucket with sand. They often seem driven to perfect their skills and to make sense of their experience. Providing for such 'play follow-up' opportunities allows them to consolidate maths concepts and language, as well as ensuring a good balance between adult and child directed activity.

Telling stories with props

Another way of making maths meaningful is telling stories with props, which focus and hold the children's attention and provide visual cues to help them understand the concepts. This is a developmentally appropriate way for practitioners to teach more directly, modelling the relevant language and often engaging the children in the problem-solving which is central to maths. After this input, the props are made available for the children to play with, thus assimilating the concepts, skills and language. More structured follow-up activities can also be provided to reinforce the learning.

Any concept can be a starting point, and the following example deals with 'recognising and recreating simple patterns'. The story requires three characters, a soil-filled tray and several red and yellow flowers made from card and straws.

> Teddy is planting flowers in his garden (the tray) in a simple pattern (red, yellow, red, yellow). Duck comes along, admires the garden and Teddy explains how he's made his pattern. They both leave, and along comes a naughty dog who picks all the flowers and leaves them in a heap. Duck returns, sees what's happened and enlists the children's help in replanting the garden in the same pattern before Teddy returns. Children enjoy hearing the stories over again, and you can extend them, for instance by making more complex patterns. Children are encouraged to have a go themselves with the flowers and other materials you provide.
>
> (Faust 2004)

Such stories can be simplified for younger children or made more complex for those who are older or more experienced. Above all, told stories provide a meaningful context which helps children make sense of new and complex information about their world. Research such as that in Margaret Donaldson's *Children's Minds* (1978) has shown the importance of framing what we present to young children in ways that engage and focus their attention and make 'human sense'. Martin Hughes (1986a) wrote:

> We have on our side ... a strength that is often underestimated: the immense capacity of young children to grasp difficult ideas if they are presented in ways which interest them and make sense to them ...

It is worrying to see the many published activities which appear to have no meaning or interest for young children. A few years ago the 'National Numeracy Strategy' published a set of activities for Foundation Stage children which contained some very inappropriate suggestions. One recommended teaching children about length in a class group by demonstrating how to measure a ribbon using crayons, for no apparent reason. If instead a story was told about a Teddy who wanted some new ribbon for her hat to go to a wedding, inviting the children to solve the problem by trying out different lengths, children would be more likely to engage and learn.

Subject knowledge and understanding child development

If you are working with young children, it is important to know about early mathematics as well as how children's understanding develops. For instance, it is helpful to know the different meanings that a '3' can represent:

There are 3 little pigs in this story.
The story starts on page 3.
There's the number 3 bus.

The first statement relates to a cardinal number that is a set or group of things, while the second uses the ordinal number because it is about the order of pages in the book, three being between two and four. When we use 'first, second, third' and so on, we are also using ordinal numbers. The last statement is different again, because 3 is the name or label of the bus. This matters because it gives us insight into the complexity of understanding about numbers for the young child, who has to work out which meaning applies. Haylock and Cockburn (1989) point out that:

> at a very early age the child encounters one enormous difficulty that runs right through mathematics: that one symbol is used to represent vastly different situations.
>
> (Haylock and Cockburn 1989: 23)

Often children will be focused on one meaning, as we can see in the example of the 4-year-old who was baking cakes with his mother. She asked him how many of the six cakes would be left if they ate four, and he replied 'five and six', much to her surprise. It seems he was attending to ordinal number, when the expected response involves cardinal number (take four away from a set of six cakes, leaving two).

We can detect confusion when a practitioner refers to five cakes, and the child exclaims, 'but I'm three!' Not an unusual occurrence.

Many young children appear to count reliably, with one-to-one correspondence and a correct number count, but don't have a grasp of the cardinal principle. This means that they don't understand that the last number in the count represents the number of items in the group. They often appear to think that counting is about recitation rather than finding out how many items there are. So it's important for practitioners to say 'so there are seven cakes on the plate' after counting to seven.

Another difficulty for many children is developing an understanding of abstract maths. Martin Hughes (1986b: 15, article in Child Education) asked Patrick, a 4-year-old,

> 'How many is two and one more?
> Four
> How many is two lollipops and one more?
> Three
> How many is two elephants and one more?
> Three
> How many is two giraffes and one more?
> Three
> So how many is two and one more?
> Six'.

As long as the numbers relate to concrete, if imaginary items, many young children can add up, but if they are totally abstract, they cannot do it. Hughes believes the difficulty lies with 'the new and difficult language of maths' and that children need a lot of help with this.

As well as understanding such developments, and helping children to progress, practitioners need to combine high expectations with a lack of pressurising. In other words, if a child is interested in recording her age of three and a half, it is important to help her with this, but it would be inappropriate to teach a whole group about fractions.

The EPPE research has emphasised that practitioners need to have subject knowledge as well as knowledge of child development, and while this is true, it seems likely that the latter is more important than the former in the early years. The maths involved is not advanced, but the ability to understand what the child is thinking mathematically and how to support and extend this depends on experience, sensitivity and understanding of how very young children learn and develop.

The Williams Report (2008) recommendation that there should be 'at least one mathematics specialist in each primary school with a deep subject knowledge', even with the proviso that she/he has a comprehensive understanding of 'the pedagogy for mathematical learning in the EYFS', could thus be problematic for nursery and reception classes. Those who are not early years specialists tend to underestimate the training, expertise and experience necessary to work effectively with this age group. Primary mathematics specialists may not have this knowledge and ability, and *'pedagogy for mathematics in the EYFS'* cannot be acquired easily without an in-depth knowledge of child development. For instance, really understanding exactly how young children learn through play takes a great deal of study and experience. The added recommendation that 'ITT entry qualifications should not distinguish between the primary and early years sectors' is also ill advised, as there is rarely time to cover both in depth, and the early years sector invariably becomes marginalised.

It makes more sense for early years practitioners, who of course are sometimes involved with the whole birth to five years age range, to have good initial training in what has now become known as 'problem-solving, reasoning and numeracy', focusing on birth to five, as well as continuing support and development. Primary maths specialists would be less likely to impose a developmentally inappropriate curriculum on young children if they work in partnership with EYFS practitioners who are well trained in early year's maths and understand what is developmentally appropriate.

References

Donaldson, M. (1978) *Children's Minds*, London: Fontana.

The Early Years Mathematics Group (1997) *Learning Mathematics in the Nursery: Desirable Approaches*, Malton: BEAM.

Faust, H. (2004) *Animated Stories for Young Mathematicians*, Malton: BEAM.

Haylock, D. and Cockburn, A. (1989) *Understanding Early Years Mathematics*, London: PCP.

Hughes, M. (1986a) *Children and Number*, Oxford: Blackwell.

Hughes, M. (1986b) 'Bridge that gap', *Child Education*, February.

Inkpen, M. (1992) *Kipper's Toybox*, London: Hodder Children's Books.

Karmiloff-Smith, A. (1994) *Baby It's You*, London: Ebury Press.
Pound, L. (1999) *Supporting Mathematical Development in the Early Years*, Oxford: Oxford University Press.
Sutton, E. (1973) *My Cat Likes to Hide in Boxes*, London: Puffin.
Williams, P. (2008) *Independent Review of Mathematics Teaching in Early Years Settings and Primary Schools*, London: DCSF.
Worthington, M. and Carruthers, E. (2003) *Children's Mathematics: Making Marks, Making Meaning*, London: PCP.

Further reading (children's)

Browne, E. (1994) *Handa's Surprise*, London: Walker Books.
Carter, D. A. (1987) *How Many Bugs in a Box?* London: Orchard Books.

As you read through this long and thoughtful chapter you will see the links with much that has already been discussed in this book – the value of play, the importance of tuning in to what it is the child is paying attention to, understanding schematic behaviour and so on. There is so much to think about! Now read the case studies that follow to see children solving problems and developing theories.

Chapter 16

Tricks

Maria Figueiredo

Maria Figueiredo was a student on the Early Childhood Studies Scheme at the University of North London when she wrote these observation notes relating to her work as a childminder with 6-year-old Louis. All young children also start to use one thing to stand for or represent another and this is an important aspect of learning, since so many of our systems are symbolic.

Louis is learning the times tables and his teacher taught him what he called a 'trick' to work out when the 9 times table is correct (the pattern for the 9 times table is 9, 18, 27, 36, 45 and so on and you will quickly notice that the first digit goes up by 1 while the second digit goes down by 1). He found it very interesting and, as a result, was convinced that he could find other 'tricks' to work out the other tables. All throughout the following week, holding paper, pencil and a calculator, Louis was determined to find a similar 'trick' for the other tables. From time to time he would come up to me, very excited, saying that he had found the trick, but when he started to explain it to me he began to realise that it did not work. I observed him adding, subtracting, making up new rules, checking the results in order to get his trick right. By the end of the week his enthusiasm had begun to fail.

Despite his obvious disappointment, his willpower helped him carry on trying. In the following week he came up to me, extremely excited, because he had finally found a 'trick' for the 5 times table. His explanation of his newly found 'trick' was accurate and clear, which showed he had worked on it a great deal.

This is how he explained it. 'Imagine you are doing 5×4. Now 4 is an even number, so for even numbers you break them into half and then add a zero to the number. See?' He held up the paper to me so I could see his work.

$$5 \times 4 = ?$$
$$4/2 = 2$$
$$2 \text{ add a } 0 = 20$$

I was amazed and replied 'Well done!' Louis continued. 'Now listen carefully because the odd numbers are harder. Imagine we are doing 5×3. Now 3 is the number you are going to work on, so this time you go for the number before

3 which is 2. Then break it into half, which is 1 and add a 5 to it, which makes it 15!'

Louis was clearly paying attention to rules and patterns and since he was following up something he had learned in the formal setting of school through his chosen explorations (i.e. through play) he reveals the very sophistication of his thinking.

In the next set of observations we find another young child developing theories of his own. As you read it, pay attention to the role of the adult.

Chapter 17

'Let's make honey!'

Mary Smith

Mary Smith worked at one of Islington's Under Fives Centres and was studying at the time she made these observation notes. She focused on 4-year-old Daniel and managed to tune into his interests – to share his focus of attention. She describes what happened in the garden of the Centre as the result of a swarm of bees arriving in it.

A group of two girls and four boys is looking at a small swarm of bees that arrived this spring in our garden, next to the large climbing frame on the grass bank. The bees have made lots of holes in this part of the garden. They go in and fly out all day long. At first the children observing them were a little scared, saying things like 'They're monsters!' and screaming, then running away, and then returning for another look. One of the boys, Daniel (4 years, 6 months) asked if they were wasps or bees and wanted to know if they could make honey. Together we took a closer look and decided they were the wrong colour for wasps and were also too big. Aaron (3 years, 6 months) said they were monsters and then tried to shoot them with his finger, going 'zap zap' from a safe distance! Daniel was still looking at them and started talking about making honey. He said we could make some at the nursery. I asked him how we could do it. He replied that we had to pick some flowers together★. We went inside to get a tray for the flowers, then back to the garden to collect wild flowers – daisies, buttercups and dandelions. When the tray was full we sat on the grass and studied them. Daniel said, 'We have to pick out the pollen from the centre of each flower'.★ It took a while to do this, placing it in the corner of the tray. Daniel said we had enough to make the honey and then asked me go get a cup and spoon. I got them. Daniel put the contents into the cup and then stirred it with the spoon saying, 'I know it will make honey'★.

After a time I asked, 'What's happening to it, Daniel?' 'Nothing', he replied, 'We have to add apple juice to it and then it will be honey'★ – I got the apple juice from the kitchen. Daniel poured it into the cup and stirred, saying, 'Is it honey now?'

'No', I replied. 'I don't think people can make honey … only bees'. Daniel was not convinced and said, 'We have to put more pollen in and then it will be honey'★. We added more, but couldn't make honey. At this point I said, 'Daniel, we've tried our best to make honey, but people can't make it. We'll look for a book about bees and that will show us how they make it'. We found a book and sat for a long time reading, looking and explaining – page by page. As a follow-up we went to the shop to buy honey and even managed to get a jar with honeycomb in it. The children enjoyed the experience of spreading the honey on rolls and eating them at tea time.

Note: * Indicates how Daniel has developed a theory about how to make honey.

Chapter 18

Making ice

Sarah Cotter

Sarah Cotter was working in one of Camden's nurseries and studying part-time when she wrote this piece. In it she describes what happened after the children had listened to the story, 'Bear's Long Walk Home', which describes a walk in the snow and which mentions icicles and 'frozen steam'. Like Mary in the previous piece, Sarah took advantage of something happening to extend the children's learning – i.e. a spell of very cold weather. But her starting point for the activity was a story.

I wanted to relate the activity to the story and wanted to try and freeze water outside and not in the freezer. The weather was very cold. Two bowls were put on the table with a jug of water.

'What do you think happens to water if it gets very cold?' I asked.
'It goes like ice', Michael said.
Rebecca asked, 'Can we make water go cold and see if it turns to ice?'
I replied that that was what I wanted to try. The children poured some water into the bowls: more in one than the other. Michael and Rebecca carried the bowls outside. The next morning the children eagerly asked what had happened to their bowls of water. Michael and Rebecca fetched them.
Rebecca said, 'Look! Look! Mine's not water anymore'.
Michael brought his in and said, 'Mine's not like Rebecca's'.
Rebecca looked at Michael's bowl and said, 'You've got too much water'.
'But it was cold outside', said Michael. While saying this he put his hand into the bowl. 'Look, I have got some hard water'.
'Ice, silly!' said Rebecca.
'But I've got cold water underneath', said Michael.
I asked Rebecca what she thought she would find if she broke the top of her ice. 'I don't know. I can try', she said. I gave her a fork and she started breaking up the ice. 'It's all ice', she said.
That's right', I replied. 'You had less water so it all got cold enough to freeze. Michael had more water in his bowl so the top got cold enough to freeze, but the rest of it didn't'.

Rebecca asked if we could add hot water to the ice to see what happened. I went and got some hot water and poured it slowly for the children to see.

'The ice has gone', Michael said.

'The hot water warmed it up and melted it', I explained.

'Can I feel it?' Rebecca asked.

I tested it first to make sure it wasn't too hot.

When Rebecca felt it she said, 'Mummy says I'm like hot and cold water'.*

'What do you mean?' I asked. 'Hot and cold make warm water, like black and white skin make brown skin, like me'.

Sarah Cotters commented on the observation as follows:

The story I used as the starting point for this activity clearly introduced scientific concepts to the children. However, for them to understand these they needed the opportunity to explore for themselves. Early on in the activity I provided an opening question which demonstrates a 'cognitive demand': 'What do you think happens when water gets very cold?' The answer Michael gave, 'It goes like ice', is scientific. If Michael had not been given that information from the story he may not have come up with that answer. So Michael may have been drawing on his previous experience of ice or on his understanding of the story.

Later I used the skills of observing, understanding, and listening to be able to collect the children's findings and help them come to a conclusion. For the children it was a fun learning experience, finding out about hot, cold, hard, soft and quantity. The links Rebecca made between hot and cold and black and white show how children always draw on real-life experiences. The children were interested in the activity and talked through it, offering ideas, suggestions and comments and, in Rebecca's case, using talk to demonstrate her feelings of being special.

Note: * Rebecca's comment about the mixing of hot and cold and the mixing of black and white is a moving example of a child showing awareness and appreciation of difference and individuality.

Part V

Understanding the written world

All of our young children live in a world where the written word is prominent. They see words written all around them – in shops, on street signs, on food packets, on television, in books. They encounter people reading these words – sometimes for pleasure, sometimes for information, sometimes for other purposes. As young children struggle to make sense of their world, they try to understand just what it is the adults they see around them are doing when they 'engage with print'. Because the development of early literacy is so important, this is a very long section. It is made up of key chapters by Henrietta Dombey and Gillian Lathey, and supported by case studies and their follow-up.

Chapter 19

It all starts with /c/ /a/ /t/ – or does it?

Foundation phonics

Henrietta Dombey

This part opens with a seminal chapter, written by **Henrietta Dombey**, from the University of Brighton. She looks at the teaching and learning of reading (and writing) in early years classes in England. In doing this, she examines the current trend of placing a tremendous emphasis on the teaching of 'synthetic phonics' but does that within a deep understanding of linguistics, literacy and culture. This is a very long and detailed chapter, but what is said is so important and thought-provoking that you are invited to read it all and enjoy it as much as I did.

Working with letters and sounds in a reception classroom

We're in a Reception class in a south coast town. It's not a wealthy area – the school scores high on the index of social deprivation. And between them, the children have 33 home languages in addition to English. It's just after the summer half-term and the children are well practiced in their phonics. They were taught three letters a week in the autumn term, and since the New Year, have been consolidating these and working with blends and digraphs. Winston Wolf (the puppet) who has been helping them throughout the year, is now sitting on a shelf, under the alphabet frieze, which is augmented with blends and digraphs.

While the other children in the class engage in self-chosen activities, a group of five sits round a table with their teacher, Louise. 'Ready for robot arms?', she asks. 'Are you listening? Here come the sounds'. She swings her arms stiffly, alternately left and right, pronouncing the phonemes /sh/, /i/ and /p/, one phoneme to each arm swing. The children put them together and shout 'ship', most with ease and all with evident enthusiasm. Next they do 'chop', 'cat' and 'fish' with similar success. Then Louise consults a record sheet, and asks Annie to do 'posh', Marty to do 'chip' Andrea to do 'boat', Maria to do 'shop' and Pavel to do 'chap'.

Now she says 'You're going to help me find some letters'. As instructed, they find the plastic letters 'a', 'e' 'i', 'o' and 'u' from a pile on the table. 'Now we need the letters 'r', 'p', 'f' and 't',' she says, pronouncing them phonically. To the group of letters in front of them, she adds cards with 'ch' and 'sh' written boldly on them. All the other letters go back in the box. She reminds the children to tap out each phoneme in the words they are about to spell. Looking at her record sheet again, she says "tap', so we go like this /t/ /a/ /p/', placing a finger on the table as each phoneme is pronounced. 'Can you do it, Annie?' Annie can, the others agree she got it right and the sense of achievement is palpable.

These children are being taught phonics effectively and enthusiastically by a highly skilled teacher. They are a good bit 'further on' than their predecessors were at a similar age, only a few years ago. They are confidently handling vowel and consonant digraphs, and some of them at least are adept at blending consonants to 'read' and write words such as 'glad' and 'trip'. They have also learned a number of 'tricky' words as 'one-offs', such as 'the' and 'was', so they do not have to be confined to stilted 'decodable' texts of the 'Nan can fan Dan' variety.

Other aspects of reading and writing are not totally neglected in this classroom. There is a well-filled book corner, although no-one is using it at the moment. The children are read to every day and take at least three books home every week, some for family members to read to them, some for them to read to family members. There's also a writing table, but not much evidence of its use. So are these children well on the road to becoming fluent and effective readers and writers? Are their teachers making best use of the Foundation Stage?

Much of the enthusiasm so evident with the children disappears when we go into the headteacher's office. She's proud that the children have a much better grip on phonics than their predecessors, but says that getting them to apply this knowledge in writing is still a challenge. And their reading is less successful than their writing. 'Children aren't using picture clues any more. It takes longer for them to get into what a story is saying. I sometimes get the feeling that we're not communicating what reading and writing are for'.

Certainly writing seems to be less often put to use for the children's own purposes. There's a notice saying 'no smocing' in the café the children have made in the role-play area. But they mostly write dictated lists of regular words, dictated sentences making use of such words, perhaps connected to a story they have been read, or to other work going on in the classroom. The classroom has no letterbox, and the children are not used to writing messages or stories for others to read, with or without the help of more experienced writers. Shared story writing doesn't feature here.

Reading in this classroom is more a matter of practising phonics than enjoying what a text has to say. Very few children go readily to the book corner to 'talk their way through a book'. It's all too understandable that they don't make use of picture cues when asked to read. Reading for these children is sounding and blending. They are learning how to use the phonic toolkit, with little idea of what they might make with it. The trouble is, that unlike Swedish, Swahili, Spanish, Italian and many other spelling systems, English has a devilishly complex phonic toolkit that takes a long time for most children to acquire and even longer for them to learn to use with ease. Postponing reading and writing for their own purposes until they are fully competent decoders and spellers means that many children labour for years to do something they see little point in.

So what should we do?

We have to admit that:

- nostalgia is dangerous – there were never more than a few classrooms in which young children were given a rich sense of the power and purposes of written language
- young children are capable of learning sound/symbol relationships more rapidly and at an earlier age than we used to believe
- such learning can be pleasurable to them and give them a sense of achievement
- without doubt, the lessons they learn about our writing system, as their teachers put into practice the contents of Letters and Sounds, the Primary National Strategy's comprehensive handbook on phonics teaching (Department for Education and Skills, DfES 2007), make an important contribution to becoming a fluent reader of an alphabetic language
- as well as the phonic knowledge they are acquiring, these children are learning a measure of self-reliance, and that effort pays off.

But the pay-off could be even more rewarding if the children had a richer experience of putting reading and writing to use in these early years and if they were allowed to use two other strategies when encountering new words in running text – analogy and guessing from pictures and context.

English spelling and the strategies appropriate for it

'Sounding out', letter by letter doesn't always work in English. We need to look at the nature of English spelling here. As we all know to our cost, it is not easy to learn to read and write in English. 'Breaking the code' isn't just a matter of learning to match 26 letters to their corresponding speech sounds and then, hey presto! You can read! We need to think carefully about how we teach children to read English, not pretend it's like Italian.

Learning to read in Italian, at least at the start, is actually pretty straightforward for two reasons. Most Italian words are simply structured, ending in vowels, and the 25 phonemes of spoken Italian are represented by 24 alphabetic letters and eight two letter combinations (such as 'ch' which is always like our 'ch' in 'choir'). The Italians are lucky to have what is termed a transparent or shallow orthography (writing system), which means that there is a consistent set of relationships between the phonemes of Italian and the letters that represent them. So perhaps it's not surprising that most Italian children master the basics of reading after only 6 months of schooling (Cossu et al. 1995).

The problem with English is twofold. First, English words are more complex than most Italian words in terms of their phonemic composition (the speech sounds that make them up). English words are full of consonant blends, as in 'strength' and 'cramp' for example. As Ziegler and Goswami (2005) have shown, languages like this are harder to learn to read than languages where most spellings follow the c+v+c+v pattern, with words like 'pizza' and 'vino'. Even if we had a more regular and consistent orthography (spelling system), our consonant clusters would make it harder to learn to read English than Italian.

But, of course we don't have a consistent spelling system: we have something much more complex. We have what is called an opaque or deep orthography. In English, there is no consistent relationship between spoken sounds and written symbols, no easy set of mapping rules to relate all spoken to all written words. If we teach children to 'sound out' every unknown word they come across, as if we had a shallow orthography like Italian, we get into difficult water. Last week I saw a group of Year 1 children trying to 'sound out' the word 'treasure'. They needed a lot of help. Not only do the vowel letters break the rules the children have learned, but also the 's' represents neither the /s/ of 'sit' nor the /z/ of 'is'. You have to know a lot of complex rules before you can work out 'treasure' on your own, if you rely on phonics to do it.

The French have a deep orthography too, but it's not as deep as ours. In French, one speech sound or phoneme, may be spelled a number of different ways (e.g. 'eau', 'oh', 'ô', 'ault, 'aud' or 'ot'). We also do this: /sh/ is spelled as 'sh' in 'sheep', etc., 's' in 'sure', 'ss' in 'passion', 'ch' in 'chef', 'c' in 'ocean' and 'special', etc., and 't' in 'station' and countless other words ending in 'ion'. Then we have the notorious triplets 'to', 'too' and 'two', and also 'soup', 'through', 'lose', 'grew', 'blue' and 'rule'. So, without including any really unusual words, we have six different spellings of the same /sh/ phoneme and nine different spellings of the same /oo/ phoneme – 15 different graphemes (that is, letters or combinations of letters representing phonemes) for those two phonemes.

However, in addition to multiple spellings of the same phoneme, in English we also have multiple pronunciations of the same spelling. So we have 'tap' and 'tall', 'lone' and 'gone', 'read' and 'read'. It tends to be the vowels that are most heavily inconsistent, as in 'The book he *read* was How to Read' and 'The cat was falling past another cat'. In that last sentence, I make it five different phonemes represented by the letter 'a' (although if you have a Northern British accent, it may be only four). Our consonants can be treacherous too, as in 'The Council agreed to house the family in a three bedroom house'.

All this is shown very clearly in the charts on the Notes for Guidance that come with Letters and Sounds (DfES 2007: 23–27). What the authors don't state is that such inconsistent phoneme/grapheme relationships mean that we should not be asking children to 'sound out' most of these words.

Why is our spelling system like this and what should we do?

Why is our spelling system as complex (or as apparently chaotic) as this? It's partly because English is a vowel-rich language. Leaving aside the diphthongs (those gliding vowels, such as the '/ow/ in 'cow', or 'ciaou', where your mouth moves as you say them), spoken Italian has five vowel phonemes, each one unambiguously represented by a single letter, whereas English has twelve, but still only five proper vowel letters. In English, the range is extended a bit by graphemes, such as 'ai', 'ea', 'ee', and 'oa', made up of two vowel letters, giving us words such as 'rain', 'team', 'street' and 'goat'. But it's more complex than that. We know about the 'Magic E' in 'take', 'like', etc. that does a similar job, making the vowel letter in front of it say its name. But that's not all.

Frequently, as in some of the examples above featuring 'a', just looking at the vowel grapheme won't tell you which phoneme is represented, even when there's no 'Magic E'. You often need to look at the consonant (or consonant combination) following the vowel grapheme to determine its pronunciation. It's the 'st' in 'past' and 'most' that shows us how the 'a' and 'o' are pronounced. In the words 'cat', 'cast' and 'call', the letter 'a' represents three distinct phonemes. The 'st' and the 'll' tell us what the sound should be. If we swap the initial 'c' for another consonant, the pattern tends to hold.

Our children have more to learn in learning to read English and teachers have more to teach than their counterparts in many other countries. Yet, despite the complexity of our spelling system, in the UK in general and in England in particular, until recently, we were actually not bad at teaching reading. This is shown in the PIRLS assessments of reading in a range of developed countries, even when our children are compared with other countries with more transparent orthographies (Mullis et al. 2003). This was no mean achievement.

In most of the classrooms where those children learned the early stages of reading, their teachers were encouraging them to use other strategies for word identification in addition to phonics. Of course many words were and still are taught as sight words. Letters and Sounds (DfES 2007) recognises that 'the' 'was', 'one' and 'two' don't respond well to a phonic approach and usefully refers to them as 'tricky words'. Foundation and KS1, classroom walls are full of such words. Children are, quite rightly, taught to recognise them as whole words. But this doesn't help children work out other words that are unfamiliar on the page and may be similarly problematic.

Two useful supplementary strategies

Rhyme and analogy

The first is rhyme and analogy. When trying to work out a word, phonics should be the first approach. But if they get stuck, if the 'sounding out' process doesn't result in a recognisable word, children should be encouraged to think whether they know a word that's like the problem word in front of them.

The most consistent and useful patterns are rhyme/rime patterns, where the consonants following the vowel tell you how it should be pronounced. Here it's useful to think of words not as sequences of individual phonemes, but in terms of the slightly larger units of onsets and rimes. The onset is the part of a one syllable word that comes before the first vowel. The rime is what follows it. So the rime of street' is 'eet' as in 'feet' and 'meet'.

Many words that can't be 'sounded out' in classic fashion, phoneme by phoneme fall into rhyming groups, with consistent spelling patterns, such as 'fast and 'past', 'cold' and 'sold'. This provides children learning to read with a second strategy, a second string to their bow. If children know 'fast' and also know about how words can be grouped in rhyming patterns, then, when they come across 'last' or 'past', they can be encouraged to draw an analogy with the familiar 'fast'. 'You know 'fast', so I bet you can read this one!' you can say to a reader towards the end of the Reception year.

But this useful rhyme tool will only be available to our children if we:

- help them become sensitive to rhyme through rhyming games in nursery classes and other early year's settings
- group words that rhyme and share the same rime in reception classes (e.g. 'cat', 'fat', etc. 'ball', 'call', etc.)
- encourage children in reception classes to look for patterns.

To do this systematically, we need to train children to recognise key rhymes by presenting useful groups of rhyming words, first orally, then orally and visually. The lists of rhyming words should not be exhaustive: the point is that the rhyme and analogy strategy enables children to recognise words they haven't come across before, so you don't put every rhyming word on the list. And you don't need to list every group of such words. Once you've drawn their attention to 'call' and 'fall', you might try 'roll' and 'toll'.

Guessing in context

This is the second supplementary strategy, the third string to the young reader's bow. Where a word such as 'lose' defeats the young reader, who can neither 'sound it out' nor find an appropriate already familiar analogy, it is surely permissible to make a careful guess in context. Re-reading up to the problem word with an expectant intonation, and articulation of the initial letter can often help. So can reading past (or beyond) the problem word, before returning to it. I should say a few words here about accuracy and momentum. In a wonderfully subtle study of 26 children learning to read, Bussis and colleagues (1985) showed that while some of the 5- and 6-year-olds read with momentum at the expense of accuracy, others were overconcerned with accuracy at the expense of momentum. Our job as teachers is to give children the tools to do both – that is we have to ensure they develop the knowledge they need for reading with accuracy and the commitment to making text mean that they need for momentum to develop. And of course we need to help them achieve a balance between these two drives.

Careful guessing in context supports the drive for momentum. But it should be held in check by examination of the beginning grapheme and by careful consideration of the fit with the established context. So in: 'The frog said he might lose it':

- children in reception might be expected to have learned 'the' and 'said' as 'tricky words'
- they might work out 'frog' phoneme by phoneme
- then they could tackle 'might' using the analogy of 'night'.

When the other two strategies are exhausted, they should be encouraged to guess what the frog might do with 'it', checking any guesses against what has gone on in the story thus far and that initial letter 'l'.

Of course we can help this process by re-reading the text up to the problem word, with an expectant intonation, and articulating the initial 'l'. We could also preface this last move with a quick recap of essential information. 'This frog! He doesn't seem to manage keep anything'. 'The frog said he might l_____ it'.

This may sound complex, but it doesn't seem so to children when they put it into practice. If you watch them carefully, you'll find it's what the better readers in your class are doing already.

And what are the alternatives?

- Children could wait until they get to the phonic rule that states that 'igh' is pronounced like a long /i/ and still be baffled by 'lose'.
- They could wait for someone to tell them both 'might' and 'lose'.

If children are to become independent readers, extending their experience of reading and so improving their skill, they need to use the strategies that will help them identify words for themselves. Synthetic phonics on its own won't do this effectively for children learning to read in English.

So what should we be doing in nursery and reception classes to help children along this path?

First, we should make all activities connected with reading as pleasurable as possible. We are not going to serve our children well if we turn them against the whole business at an early age. So phonic games, and *Letters and Sounds* (DfES 2007), is full of them, are definitely a good idea where they are games and not thinly disguised tasks. There is no doubt that helping children to develop an awareness of speech as a sequence of sounds and helping them establish firm connections between phonemes and the graphemes that most straightforwardly represent them is of great benefit. But it's unrealistic to expect most children to decode much text for themselves until towards the end of the reception year. We should not be in the business of setting children up for failure. Instead we should remind ourselves that many of the countries whose children score above ours on international tests at nine or so start to teach reading when the children are six or seven.

We should also remind ourselves that learning to read is hard work that involves rewiring the brain, establishing connections along pathways that are not fully myelinated (equipped with a sheath that speeds communication) until they are around five (Wolf 2008). And if children are to invest the energy into it that the process requires, they should feel that they are getting something out of the process. So we need not only to make the phonic games and alphabet friezes fun, we also need to make use of written text throughout the day in ways that are rewarding for children.

Pleasure in reading and experience of it

The sad fact is, that although (at least until relatively recently) our children have scored well on international studies of reading competence at around 9 years (Mullis et al. 2003), they score significantly less well than others in comparable countries in terms of their attitudes to reading. Our children like reading much less than their counterparts in Sweden, Bulgaria and a host of other countries. Studies carried out in England show a marked decline in children's liking for reading over the last 12 years or so (Sainsbury 2004). We don't have the same information on writing, but I suspect that writing too has become less popular with children in England over this time.

And if children don't like reading, they don't do it when they don't have to. This means that they don't get better at it and may even lose some of their reading skill over time.

Meanwhile, the lure of visual media grows ever stronger. Young children may spend over 4 hours a day in front of computer screens, where it's unlikely they'll be involved in much reading. And even if they do pick up books, they may well not be reading the written text. Reference books for children and adults are increasingly visual, leading some children (particularly boys) to focus on the pictures alone, neglecting the written text. None of these aspects of modern life is essentially harmful. But if we want our children to read, to engage in the personal world-building and the considered choice-making that make up a richly informed life, then we have to work hard to teach them to experience reading as rewarding from the start. The same goes for writing.

So one essential thing we have to do in the nursery and reception years is to build an interest in, a passion for, and a commitment to reading and writing.

What young children need to learn

Children learn to talk through being involved in conversation, being given turns, listened to and responded to. They don't learn by being taught all the phonemes of spoken English, one at a time, with no real involvement in communication until they know all 44. Instead the most successful learners are engaged in complex interactions from a very early stage, encouraged and supported in the business of building meaning through language.

Of course we can take this parallel too far. Learning written language is not like learning spoken language. There's not the same pressing communicative need and it doesn't happen as easily for most children. Very few children fail to learn to talk. Our brains may be wired for us all to learn to talk, but they are certainly not wired for us to learn to read: we have to do some very deliberate learning, laying down a mass of new pathways between very different parts of the brain if we are to learn to read fluently (Wolf 2008).

What this means is that we need to recognise that there are two sides to learning to read: the technical business of 'decoding' or identifying written words and the business of using those words to communicate and think with. The same is true for writing. Of course, in both cases, there is an interaction between the technical and the meaningful aspects. As I said earlier, the more a child reads, the better he gets at word identification, so readers who are keen on finding out what written texts have to offer become more efficient at identifying words. The converse is also true: those who can decode words easily are in a better position to attend to the meaning of what they are reading. And this holds true for writing as well as reading. Children's experience of reading and writing needs to involve both aspects, from the start through to the point where all technical aspects have been mastered.

Not so long ago, there were few books in UK nursery classes, and certainly no attempt was made to teach reading or writing. Then the books came in, and a greater emphasis was given to experience with books – to the teacher reading aloud, to the teacher or other adult reading with a small group and to children's own self-initiated encounters with books. But sounds and letters were not introduced until reception or Year 1 (the first years of formal education). Now there's an almost desperate rush to get children 'reading' regular three and four letter words at least before the end of Reception. The books may still be there, but experience of making sense of them has taken something of a back seat.

As well as ensuring that the phonic activities are enjoyable, we need to redress the balance in the Foundation Stage. We need to start from the assumption that written language is a channel of communication that children should be encouraged to make use of, for their own purposes, from the very beginning. At the same time we shouldn't throw out all the phonic learning developed over recent years. We need to help children become aware of speech as a sequence of sounds, a sequence that is capable of being divided up into words and even smaller units, and that these smaller units can be matched with letters. And we must help children relate their growing knowledge of words and letters to the business of making meaning from text.

What can we learn from the learners?

First, we need to recognise the most important people in the classroom – the children. Some will start in an early years setting having experienced over a thousand story-readings in English with parents or carers. Others will come with a similar experience in other languages. Still others may come having enjoyed books shared in lively ways at SureStart sessions, some involving their parents in practices that have now spread to their homes. All these children will have learned forms of book language, different from the everyday language of conversation. They will have learned the patterning of stories and what to expect of them. They will have come to understand that there's more to the world than they have learned from their first-hand experience – and that books can help them travel in their imagination far beyond the confines of home and school.

But some children will have had very little of such shared book experience. Yet, such experience makes a key contribution to the ease and success with which children learn to read. Given the complexity of English spelling discussed above, this experience is perhaps particularly important for children learning to read English, so that they taste some of the rewards that reading can give, before they are asked to work the words out by themselves.

And then of course, there's the digital technology. Nearly all children come to the nursery or setting with a wide experience of electronic equipment – of mobiles and TV remotes as well as computer games. Play with these may have familiarised them with keyboards and the forms of letters, as well as numbers. Some may even manage simple operations at the computer.

I've already discussed the other key experience for promoting literacy learning – experience of speech sounds (phonemes) and the letters of the alphabet that most straightforwardly represent them. The children who arrive at school with an awareness of 20 speech sounds and of the letters that can represent these are better placed to learn to read and write.

Giving children the experiences they need

Our job in the Foundation Stage is to build on children's preschool experience. This means introducing children new to books to their power and fascination, while deepening and widening the experience of those already familiar with books. It's vital that books become a source of joy, wonder and comfort, rather than mere recognition of the mundane words of a mundane storyline.

It also means helping children who have little awareness of letters or speech sounds develop such an awareness and helping those more advanced in this aspect of literacy learning extend the range of their phonic knowledge and put it to use in making sense of texts.

So Foundation classes need alphabet friezes, 'sound books', magnetic letters and whiteboards – all vital sources of information to help children begin to get to grips with English spelling. These can be used in carefully structured games, as set out in *Letters and Sounds* (DfES 2007). They should be phased to relate to the children's current letter–sound knowledge, consolidating the existing knowledge and introducing the new.

I won't dwell on this side of literacy learning because it is the one that is currently receiving most attention. But I would like to make a few points about making early phonics effective:

- Make it playful. Keep the activities short (15 minutes is probably enough) and frequent (daily, at least).
- Involve bodily movement and physical sensation in representing speech sounds, tracing letter shapes, etc. These help lay down enduring memory patterns.
- Encourage the children to be the arbiters of right and wrong, either with other children (this will need to be carefully managed) or with puppet 'helpers', such as Winston Wolf, who wants to get things right but has a tendency to make mistakes. It can also help you to keep the children on their toes if you 'read things wrong' and encourage them to correct you.
- Ask a child who has identified a word 'Why do you think it says that?' This makes the child reflect and consider his/her reasons, and also makes the other children aware of productive strategies to and get the children to correct her/him.
- Make use of song, rhythm and rhyme. These have been rather neglected in recent years, but have much to offer. Children tend to find songs easy to remember and enjoyable to sing. Rhythm is another important aid to memory. And it's easier for children to recognise rhymes in words than individual phonemes.
- There's a mass of material on the market claimed to teach phonics. Be warned: much of it is of dubious value, as are some 'traditional' activities. I remember many years ago, seeing a reception class busy with scrunched up tissue paper which they were gluing to cardboard, cut into hook shapes. I was baffled, as were the children, although they were enjoying the glue. When I asked the teacher for enlightenment, she told me confidently that this was phonics. They were all making /j/ shapes.
- A number of computer games seem to be almost as unhelpful. Others provide drill in phonics that may connect with what you are teaching the children. But you will need to keep a close eye to see how the children use it.

You must ask yourself:

- Is the material or activity attractive?
- Is it practical to use?
- What is it teaching children?
- Is it teaching them:
  o phonological awareness (awareness of speech as sound, including awareness of rhyme)
  o letter identification
  o matching of speech sounds to letters
  o blending speech sounds to make spoken words
  o splitting words up into their component phonemes
  o matching these to letters or groups of letters?

If it is doing none of the above, like the glued on tissue paper, it's not helping children learn phonics.

- Put phonics to use throughout the day. If you're working in England, Letters and Sounds is likely to be your guide to phonics teaching and learning in your classroom. You may also be using a scheme such as Jolly Phonics. But carrying out the prescribed activities in the set order is not enough. Whenever the occasion arises in the course of the day, to demonstrate how phonic knowledge is put to use, you need to revisit lessons the children have already encountered. Otherwise there's a tendency for children to see being good at phonics as unconnected with reading. So it is important to talk about letters at relevant moments throughout the day. 'Carla's name needs to go here. It starts with a /c/, like Cal's, doesn't it. Can we find the /c/ on the alphabet frieze?'
- Don't let phonics take over every literacy activity. This may sound like a contradiction of the last point, but it's not. Phonics should help us lift words off the page and set words down. It's an aid to the construction of meaning and should not get in the way of making meaning. So make sure that you communicate to the children that finding out what happens and thinking about it are what stories are about, and that working the words out lets you do that. To use stories as a quarry for exercises in word identification is to kill the goose that lays the golden eggs. Phonics must be the servant of reading, not its master.

Making sense from written texts

The classroom should be a place where young children extend their sense of their own identity as well as their knowledge of the world and the other people in it. Literacy learning should be more than a set of skills and activities mastered to make teacher and parents happy. Young children should experience literacy as a powerful means of finding out about the world and how it works, the lives and dreams of others, the hopes and fears we share and of organising practical life. They should develop a sense of how the written word pervades the world they know. There follow some practical suggestions – some to do with making a print-rich environment, some with the activities you might promote and take part in.

A book-rich classroom

A basic need in any foundation class aimed at developing young children's literacy is, of course, a well-stocked book-corner, from which the teacher can select books for reading aloud and the children can choose books to talk their way through, on their own or in small groups. There are very many guides. *Simply the Best, 0 to 7* is available (at time of writing) from the Centre for Literacy in Primary Education, online at: www.clpe.co.uk (follow the prompts to publications). *Books for Keeps*, a magazine available six times a year, is packed with good ideas and lively reviews of recently published children's books (www.booksforkeeps.co.uk). For teacher recommendations, go to: www.sevenstories.org.uk.

The books you choose should appeal to a wide range of interests and have lively illustrations. They should encourage children to hold them, turn their pages and construct the written text from the pictures, as they talk their way through the book. The language of many of them should be memorable and bear many re-readings. Children should enjoy savouring the words in their mouths. And you should enjoy sharing the texts with them!

Writing all around

But of course, written language should not be confined to books. Drawers need labels to show what goes where. So do cupboards and coat pegs. In the nursery, these can have pictures as well as words on them, but the idea is to stress as much as possible what the written language tells us and how it helps us make the world a more orderly and reliable place.

> Look, here's where we put the Lego. It says 'Lego' on the label.

Children need to see written language in daily use – in notes, menus, lists, all made for real purposes – perhaps to remind the teacher to bring in a particular object the next day, to tell everyone what's for lunch, or to make the shopping list of the ingredients needed to make the pizza. These kinds of writing need to be shared with the children, not just taken for granted, but demonstrated, so that the children see the usefulness of the written word. In many foundation classes, the registers are arcane objects, not understood at all by the children. It's important for their literacy learning to show children what they're about, with comments such as:

> Tomas, are you having dinner today? We've got to mark it in the register, otherwise the cook won't know how much dinner to make and there might not be enough dinner for you.

Reading aloud to children

If there's one thing you can do in a Foundation classroom to promote a commitment to reading, it's reading aloud. I had a hunch about this many years ago, and time and a mass of research have proved me right. But how do you replicate the intimate home experience of parent and one or two children in a foundation setting, with 20–30 children? Small groups seem to provide the obvious answer. But the trouble is that the foundation classroom can be a very distracting place. In a buzz of competing activities, children may be lured away from the story reading before the end, and therefore lose much of its value. In some research I did in a nursery classroom, I found that it was only the one child who was regularly read to at home who would sit through a small group story from start to end, no matter who was reading it. Others would drift in after the start, or leave when they saw a chance of getting on the rocking horse.

But the whole class reading by Nicky, the teacher, was a different story. At a set time in the nursery session the children would tidy everything away, gather in front of the teacher's chair and set out with her on an imaginative journey, enlivened by the talk about the events, the characters, the words and the pictures. Some children were very vocal. 'Ooh they're not allowed in houses!' gasped Anita, shocked at the sight of the trees in Max's bedroom in *Where the Wild Things Are*. 'But the frog might push him back!' shouted Lee, when the fish lay gasping on the river bank in *Fish is Fish*. Others, like Richard, were almost completely silent for weeks, but surprisingly, showed later that they had internalised the language of stories. When he came to help one puppet 'read' a story to another, Richard managed a coherent account of Goldilocks with 23 consecutive unprompted utterances, all in the explicit language of narrative rather than the fragmentary, repetitive and implicit language of conversation.

Apart from reducing external distractions, the key to making whole class story reading an engaging experience is to make it a journey of joint discovery. The cover and the title should prompt speculation about the contents. Who's it about? Where are they? What's going to happen? How do we know? How do the characters, places and problems compare with what we know? The foundation classroom is not the place for backward looking 'comprehension' questions about what Red Riding Hood had in her basket, or how many buttons there are on Max's wolf-suit. If we are to draw all children in, including those with very little experience of story, we need to help them link the story to what they know, and enter into it as a drama.

Of course it must be read in a compelling way, with exaggerated intonation and colourful 'voices' for characters. But there are plenty of lively sound recordings that do this well. As a teacher, your job is to do something more – to make the reading personal to this group of children. You can do this partly by interjecting your own comments, such as 'D'you think he'll get her this time?' or, as Nicky said to a child in danger of distraction, 'Just fancy that, Lee! Imagine waking up in the morning and finding you'd grown two little legs in the night!'

But perhaps your most important role is to be open and responsive to the children's comments. Anita's teacher didn't ask her to be quiet, but said 'I certainly haven't got trees in my bedroom, but they've grown in the night in Max's bedroom!' And to Lee's prediction, which came after she had re-engaged him in the story, Nicky responded, 'Let's find out. Let's find out if Lee's right, if the frog will save him'. Not all children's interjections at story time are constructive. There's nearly always a child keen to tell you about the cat at home, or their nanny's dog. This is not the time to listen to such news. Try to ignore the child, or if she persists, make it clear what the accepted topic is – 'We're not talking about cats now, we're talking about wild things!' said Nicky to one persistent little girl. The key question to ask yourself is, 'Does this comment add to the children's understanding of the story?' If it does, respond to it. If it doesn't, don't. Make a mental note to catch up with the child later.

Talking books on the computer

These can play a very useful role in extending children's experience of hearing written text and making sense of it. Provided the children actually do attend to the words on the screen, they can also extend their experience of matching spoken to written words. However, there are two dangers:

• Many of the texts are excessively banal.
• Many of the programs have a distracting array of 'eye candy', such as quacking ducks that don't add to the story or teach children any useful reading lesson.

As always, ask yourself, 'What are the children learning from this experience?'

Shared reading with Big Books

Many schools have a good collection of Big Books (giant sized texts with large print that can be read from a distance) that are not much used at present. But provided the story is lively, with repetition, rhythm and/or rhyme, they are well worth getting out of the cupboard. Reading a big book together can provide a vital experience of connecting the technical side to the meaning.

In the early stages, you may want to work with easily memorable rhyming texts. You begin by reading the book aloud, then get the children to 'read' with you, sometimes pausing to work out a particular word that relates to an aspect recently taught. Sometimes, this might be a phonically regular word, such as 'bat'. Sometimes a word similar to one they already know, such as 'call', which they can work out from relating it to 'ball'.

But there may be times when you ask them to guess a word that is currently beyond them, such as 'treasure', from the context and the initial letters. In all of this you will be acting as a demonstrator, showing them what you do when you read a text, as well as an instructor, telling them what to do. Both roles have something important to contribute to their learning. This experience of sharing the process of decoding and making sense of a written text will help prepare them to use these strategies in their own reading.

Reading and writing in role-play

Role-play areas should include writing materials and appropriate reading materials too – a telephone directory beside the telephone, a TV guide, or whatever text might be appropriate to the identity of the role corner at the moment. Of course the children are unlikely to be able to read these texts in the conventional sense, but making use of them in their play develops a sense of their purpose, just as talking their way through a book develops their mastery of story language and story structure.

Some children may wish to take on the role of the teacher in the book corner. I can see Heather now, aged just four, in a nursery classroom a few years ago, sat on a chair with a book in her hand and three other girls in front of her. Using the phrasing of her teacher, Heather asks them to 'sit on your bottoms' before launching into a spirited rendition of Wanda Gag's *Gone is Gone*. It's far from word perfect, but Heather has grasped something of the books phrasing and tone as she starts. 'One day morning the little old woman came down the path …'.

It's not surprising that playing schools, along with being read to, is one of the most important preschool experiences of children who learn to read early. Role-play has the power to enable children to put different parts of their learning together and to do so in a way that fulfils their need to remake the world through their imaginations. It also teaches collaboration. Its power should not be underestimated. Playing at reading and writing enables children to try out how they feel and how they work, as well as what they can do.

A writing area

Many classes have a writing area equipped with an attractive range of pencils and paper. But what's it for? In my experience, nothing much results from this corner or table unless the teacher models its use herself for some real communicative purpose and unless a proper communicative context is created for any written language that might be produced. So instead of quietly grabbing the pen on your desk to respond to a message from another teacher, you might sometimes make a show of going to the writing area, picking a suitable instrument and piece of paper and composing your message aloud. And as for giving children a sense of purpose for their writing, Winston Wolf and friends come into their own here. Winston often leaves messages which the children find in the morning. Of course, they will need help in reading the messages, and in writing their replies, but the messages can be theirs – they can compose them, either in the whole class, or in small groups.

You might also want to set up a postal system, so children can write messages to each other. These messages should be very much the children's own, constructed without adult help. It's not a calamity if they can't initially be read at all, but it does reinforce the idea of communicative purpose and give them a pressing need to master English spelling. You can either set up a postbox, with a set delivery time, or, if each child has a shelf or box of their own, encourage them to deliver their messages to the boxes. I've seen this last system carried out very effectively with 3-year-olds in a preschool setting in Italy.

You can also encourage children to write to children in other classes, the cooks, the headteacher or even, with some adult help, to people in the world beyond school. A nursery class of 5-year-olds in a small village in a poor area of Northern Spain, complained to their teacher about the lack of play facilities in the village. She helped them write a letter to the Mayor, and they got a playground. These children had learned an important lesson about the power of the written word.

Shared writing

Like shared reading, shared writing lets children in on the business of how it's done, as nothing else can. In front of the class or group you have a whiteboard or large sheet of paper on which your story is to be written. You may suggest the topic, perhaps a notice to tell another class about a show, or an account of a walk round the school garden for the class record book. Or perhaps a child comes up with an idea. You might want to start the composition off, perhaps with 'Yesterday we all went out'. In Nursery you'd be doing most of the actual scribing of the words yourself. But in Reception, after a short time, you could start to ask the children to help you. With the first word, they might only manage the initial letter of 'yesterday', but 'we' is on the wall. The process should not be too laboured: they should feel a sense of achievement at the end, not boredom or exhaustion. A splendid book by Peter Geekie and colleagues (1999) tracks two 5-year-olds learning to write in an Australian classroom. Shared writing plays a key role in the process, showing them not only how to go about spelling, but also the kind of things you can write about.

Once you get a number of these activities going in your classroom, you'll find that others suggest themselves. The key is to focus on making written language a lived and meaningful daily experience for all the children, and not reduce it to a series of graded exercises.

Bringing it all together

Enabling children to take command of the written word is one of the most important things we do in education. We can make their entry into written language a playful, exciting and rewarding experience, in which they feel a sense of achievement from working out what the written words are saying and taste the delight of weaving words to make meaning. Or we can make it a dull and nervous affair, where children early on experience failure and develop a growing dislike of the whole process. But we should not allow ourselves to be pressured into focusing on the technical aspects at the expense of making meaning with written language. And, where small children are concerned, it's vital that we maintain responsiveness to their needs and interests instead of just delivering a pre-organised package.

References

Bussis, A., Chittenden, E., Amarel, M. and Klausner, E. (1985) *Inquiry into Meaning: An Investigation of Learning to Read*, Hillsdale, NJ: Lawrence Erlbaum.

Cossu, G., Gugliotto, M. and Marshall, J. C. (1995) 'Acquisition of reading and written spelling in a transparent orthography: two non parallel processes?' *Reading and Writing* 9: 22.

DfES (2007) *Primary National Strategy. Letters and Sounds: Principles and Practices of High Quality Phonics*, London: Department for Education and Skills.

Geekie, P., Cambourne, B. and Fitzsimmons, P. (1999) *Understanding Literacy Development*, Stoke-on-Trent: Trentham Books.

Mullis, I., Martin, M., Kennedy, A. and Flaherty, C. (eds) (2003) *PIRLS 2001 International Report: IEA's Study of Reading Literacy Achievement in Primary School in 35 Countries*, Boston, MA: Boston College, International Study Center.

Rose, J. (2006) *Independent Review of the Teaching of Early Reading: Final Report*, London: Department for Education and Skills.

Sainsbury, M. (2004) 'Children's attitudes to reading', *Literacy Today* 38: 16–17.

Ziegler, J. and Goswami, U. (2005) 'Reading acquisition, developmental dyslexia, and skilled reading across languages: a psycholinguistic grain size theory', *Psychological Bulletin* 131(1): 3–29.

There is so much to think about in this chapter that it demands several readings. So do come back to it and read it again and again. Hopefully, it will give you the ideas and language you might need to support the ways in which you are trying to create a language-rich classroom or environment.

Chapter 20

Talking in your head

Young children's developing understanding of the reading process

Gillian Lathey

Gillian Lathey is Director of the National Centre for Research in Children's Literature at Roehampton University. In this chapter, she describes a piece of research she carried out in a nursery in West London. The author was a teacher for many years and developed an interest in young children and their acquisition of literacy. Speaking two languages herself, she developed a particular interest in children's literature in translation.

As a very young child listening to stories read by his mother, Sartre tried to explain to himself what was happening. His mother lowered her eyes, appeared to fall asleep and used unfamiliar language with confidence. Who was speaking? And to whom? Sartre's conclusion was that when reading to him his mother acted as a medium, and that the book was speaking through her. When alerted by Elizabeth Plackett to this remarkable insight in Sartre's account of his early development as a reader and writer in Les Mots (1964), my decision to investigate young children's understanding of the reading process was confirmed. I hoped to find out more about what young children (3- and 4-year-olds) think the act of reading entails and how they think fluent readers process print. Having worked with young children for many years, I was quite aware that insights like Sartre's may only be momentary, and that children's perceptions of such a complex process are likely to be shifting and changing all the time. In her essay *The Development of Initial Literacy*, Yetta Goodman (1984) describes children's active search for understanding.

During early development, children may construct principles which they later have to discard. Some of these principles may actually interfere with the development of others for a period of time. The principles will overlap and interact, and the children will have to sort out which principles are most significant to meaning and which are not very useful.

The principle which the young Sartre had constructed, the delightful notion of the reader as medium, was the invention of a mind eager for understanding, and would be modified as his understanding grew.

In order to uncover some of these 'principles' constructed by young children, I spent some time in a nursery with a wide ethnic mix, close to Portobello Road in

West London, armed with picture books as well as my own reading material and a mini tape recorder. Anyone who has tried to do so will know that it is well-nigh impossible to 'interview' 3- and 4-year-olds, and that the best material is often gained by chance. After my first visit – spent entirely in the sandpit – I became a permanent fixture in the book corner for one afternoon a week ready to read stories, and to talk about books and reading when the moment seemed right. I had an agenda of questions and possible approaches, but soon found that my own personal reading material proved to be a rich source of interest, comment and speculation. I spent time reading silently and asking children for their reactions, as well as asking them to demonstrate for me what it is that silent readers do.

What goes on in a silent reader's head?

After talking about my book and reading silently for a while as a group or an individual child watched, I usually started by asking the children whether they thought I was reading or not. Responses were mixed. On two separate occasions Ben told me that he did not think I could be reading because I was not 'talking'. I then tried to find out what he thought should happen.

Me: You know when I'm reading something like this, what do you think, what do you think happens? How do I do it?
Ben: By talking like this: [He holds the book and runs his finger backwards and forwards along the flyleaf] chatter, chatter, chatter, chatter, chatter, chatter.

By his delightful use of the word 'chatter' Ben is telling me that only reading aloud counts. Like Ben, Michelle felt that I could not be reading: 'Because you're not talking'. However, later in the same afternoon I talked with Michelle about her mother reading at home. She told me that her mother read 'books, not stories' – a nice distinction! I then asked her to show me how someone at home would read a book like my novel. She held the book in both hands and commented: 'They – they would just sit quiet'. Despite her earlier answer, Michelle does know about silent reading which she has observed in her home. Even more revealing is her final comment: 'I like them being like that'. To be present while adults sit and read quietly represents for Michelle a calm and pleasant experience. Michelle's understanding of silent reading is context-dependent. Silent reading is a familiar practice at home, but in the nursery, adults always read aloud to children. My silent reading in the book corner created an artificial situation which no doubt influenced her reply.

Some children were, however, quite clear about what was happening. Hannah claimed that I was reading: 'Because you're just reading it in your head'. Samya, who was walking purposefully to another part of the nursery during one of my silent reading sessions stopped for a moment to ask in a loud voice: 'Are you talking in your head?' Alice also told me that I was reading in my head because, 'Nobody hears'. I asked her what might be going on in my head and she replied with much laughter: 'I don't know. The wheels are working'. Alice had no doubt picked up the notion of wheels going round in the head from an adult, and is glad to have a way to satisfy me! Joshua resorted to fantasy when asked the same question. He talked about a 'stick in my head'.

Me:	And what's that stick doing?
Joshua:	It's going down in your trousers and going in your shoes.
Me:	It's going down my trousers and in my shoes?
Joshua:	Yes. [touching his own legs]
Sally:	[To me] You've got tights on.

Joshua happily uses my question to allow his imagination full play, and may be thinking about puppets, or recalling a conversation about the brain sending messages through the body. Who knows? This whole conversation, including Sally's final comment, is a perfect illustration of the connections made by young children in their thinking, and how amusing and fascinating these are.

Joshua's 'stick' comment highlights the difficulty of gathering evidence in any systematic way, yet a revealing discussion on the nature of silent reading did develop quite unexpectedly, as the following scene illustrates. I am sitting in the book corner talking with Sade and looking at books. Ben and Oleuwaseun join us. I am looking at my novel.

Me:	I'm just going to read this bit to myself. You watch me. [There is an interested silence as I read.]
Me:	Now, then. Do you think I was reading that, Ben? [Ben shakes his head]
Me:	Ben doesn't think I was. Do you think … [Sade and Oleuwaseun nod]
Sade:	Yes I think you …
Me:	[to Ben] Why do you think I wasn't reading it?
Ben:	Because you weren't talking.
Sade:	No, because you didn't hear her talking.
Me:	But sometimes, you know, when grown up people read books like this, they don't talk, do they? Or do they always talk, do you think?
Sade:	No.
Oleuwaseun:	They don't have to. They can if they want.
Me:	And what do you think is going on in their head when they're reading silently like that, Seun?
Oleuwaseun:	Some people read quietly.
Sade:	They … they're reading it in their head they are.
Me:	They're reading it in their head, are they?
Sade:	In the brain. They go dm dm dm dm dm dm dm …

Me:	Do they?
Sade:	… talking …
Me:	So they're reading in their brains and it's going dm dm like that inside, is it?
Sade:	Yes.

These 3- and 4-year-olds are reflecting on the reading process as demonstrated by a fluent reader reading silently. Ben did not think that I was reading because he could hear nothing, while Sade and Oleuwaseun have a much more sophisticated understanding of what a silent reader does. Sade contradicts Ben on a fine point of logic. He should, she asserts, say simply that he did not hear me talking, not state categorically that I had not been talking at all. The thinking behind Sade's contradiction becomes clear later in the conversation. Sade states that people reading silently are reading in their heads, and then further refines 'head' to 'brain'. She even makes sounds to represent this voice in the head and describes them as 'talking'. She understands reading silently as an internalisation of the voice used when reading aloud, a voice which can be physically heard in his or her head by the reader. In order to reach such a conclusion, she must have had considerable experience of watching silent readers at work. Oleuwaseun emphasises the choice a skilled reader has – to read silently or out loud. He tells me that some people read 'quietly', but is clear that this is their choice. Both Sade and Oleuwaseun have developed an understanding that reading involves inner mental activity, and Sade makes this concrete by describing the sounds made by the voice in the brain. Nigel Hall in *The Emergence of Literacy* (1987: 32) describes how the children he talked to perceived reading as an oral activity, and some believed that even animals could learn to read and write. He found that it was not until 5 to 7 years of age that children started saying animals could not read because 'they are not human' or 'they haven't got brains'. Hall concludes:

> The idea that reading is a distinctly human activity or that it involves inner mental processing appears to be a much later development and may be due in part to instruction and an increasing metacognitive ability.
>
> (Hall 1987: 32)

I would suggest that the understanding shown by Sade and Oleuwaseun and other children who described 'reading in the head' at such a young age is unlikely to be the result of instruction, but has rather developed from experience of observing silent reading. These children are cousins, they are familiar with at least one West African language and one parent of each child is a student. They have had plenty of opportunity to observe silent reading, to watch their parents write, and to learn that it is possible to communicate in more than one language. They have, with 'increasing metacognitive ability', begun to draw their own conclusions about the processes involved in reading and no doubt in all language models.

The relationship between the reader's consciousness and print

Closely related to an understanding of what happens in a silent reader's head are children's concepts about the relationship between the reader's consciousness and print, sometimes revealed quite incidentally. On one visit to the nursery I started reading a popular picture book to a small group. Yassin walked up to us holding the model he was working on. After a while he looked at me, clearly puzzled, and asked: 'How come you know the story?' He was familiar with the book, had heard it read to him many times in the nursery and possibly at home, but was unable to understand how I, a stranger, could possibly know the same story. For Yassin the story was attached to particular people and contexts. At that moment he did not consider the story to be 'fixed' to the book, permanently there to be read by anyone. The book and the pictures were important, but somehow the story belonged to the people who told it. Unfortunately, Yassin had gone to finish his model before I could answer him or pursue the discussion further. A remark like this is a perfect opening for reflection on how books and the reading process work.

A colleague undertaking her own research, Sally Ginnever from Sir Thomas Abney School in Hackney, related a similar incident which happened in her reception class. A teacher from St Vincent had told her class a story about growing plantains. Some time after she had gone, Paul asked where the story had come from. Other children replied that it was in her head. Paul then wanted to know whether she had a book in her head! Paul's understanding appears to be the reverse of Yassin's. He may have limited experience of storytelling, and believes that stories must always be attached to books. Luckily this discussion did continue, and Sally describes how Dougal answered Paul by telling him that the teacher did not have a book in her head, but that everyone has words in his or her head and puts them together to make stories. Dougal helped Paul to begin to distinguish between story reading and storytelling by explaining to him something about the process involved in telling a story without a text.

Understanding the relationship between text and reader is an important part of learning to read, and can be a source of puzzlement for some children. Sartre's belief that the book was speaking through his mother is another example of how a child's thinking can develop, as is Alan Garner's (1980) account (in *The Signal Approach to Children's Books*) of his misunderstanding of first person narrative …

> the only time my father ever read to me was a total failure because it was 'Robinson Crusoe' and he never got beyond the third page … somewhere round there … because I kept saying 'you didn't'.
>
> (Garner 1980: 322–323)

Garner could not dissociate the words he heard from his father, who presumably made no attempt to discuss the relationship between the book and himself.

Imitating silent readers

Discussing my silent reading sessions with children revealed their developing understanding of the processes involved, as did incidental comments such as those made by Yassin and Paul. Another window onto children's thinking was opened by asking them to take my book and show me what a silent reader actually does, so that I could observe their physical gestures and actions. In their investigation into preschool children's silent reading, Ferreiro and Teberosky (1982: 155–160) found that there was a development from a belief that reading had to be accompanied by talking to an understanding of the importance of 'looking'. I asked Luca to show me how an adult would read my book. He flicked through the book and then looked hard and long at the cover and various pages, opening his eyes wide in an exaggerated fashion. On another occasion he again spent some time looking at the front cover, then looked at a page silently and uttered a loud sigh. Luca recognises the importance of looking at the book's cover to gain some idea of its content; of focusing the eyes and looking closely at the page, and of registering a reaction from time to time – in this case a sigh! Leona held my book to show me what I had been doing.

Leona: When you go like this [looking at the text in an exaggerated manner] it still means you're reading it.

Leona knows that you do not have to use your voice to read, but that 'looking' is essential.

A hypothesis which would prove to be less 'useful' (Goodman 1984) was demonstrated by several children who seemed to believe that following the text with a finger is an indispensable aspect of silent reading. I spent considerable time one afternoon with Fadua, who can speak both Arabic and English. After I had read silently, Fadua told me that she did not think I was reading, and when asked what she thought was happening she replied: 'Because you do that with your finger'. I had not been using my finger to follow the text, so presumably Fadua was implying that I ought to. Later she wanted to have a go at reading my novel, opened it at the first page and sat in silence looking at the text and running her finger slowly and carefully underneath each line. Suddenly, half way down the page she noticed a two-line quotation at the top of the page which she had not 'read' and was determined to start again. Again she sustained this 'reading' activity for a long time, until I asked a question:

Me: How did you learn – how did you know how to read like that?
Fadua: My sister knows.

Fadua then continued until she began to tire, at which point she moved faster down the page and flicked through the book looking for a page she could 'remember', the word she was using to stand for 'reading'. I wanted to investigate her understanding further, and after once more reading silently myself, asked my usual question:

Me: What do you think goes on in my head when I'm reading it? What do you think's happening when I'm reading it? You watch me. [I read silently, not using my finger.]

Fadua: cause – cause – you – fingers [speaking very slowly and deliberately]

Me: Mmmmm ... what have I got on my fingers?

Fadua: [distracted by noise] It's a bit louder – a little bit come ... over there.

Me: What happens if I'm not using my fingers?

Fadua: Because ... can't read it.

Me: I can't read it? Do I need to use my fingers?

Fadua: ?

Me: Can I read it without using my finger?

Fadua: Yes.

Fadua, through watching her older sister read, has developed the notion that following lines of print with the finger is an essential part of reading, even for silent readers. As she learns to read herself, this will no doubt be a helpful strategy for a time, but she will realise that it is not essential. Indeed she seems to change her thinking during the course of our final conversation, probably as a result of my questions. When I ask what is happening, it is the use of the finger which is her first concern. Fadua seems to be saying that I could not read without using my finger, yet when asked a direct question realises that of course, I could. Here is an instance of the development described by Yetta Goodman (1984: 105) when a child has constructed a principle which may: 'actually interfere with the development of others for a period of time'.

Fadua does not, for example, make exaggerated eye movements or mention the importance of 'looking' as other children did. She is concerned with one principle for the time being, yet her thinking is already beginning to shift. Fadua's concentration and absorption when following lines of small print were quite remarkable, as was the length of time she spent on this activity.

Conclusions

Talking with young children about their understanding of the reading process has proved to be a fascinating and often entertaining area of research. At times, my questioning forced children to invent spontaneous answers (the 'gems' we all love to hear), and in some cases acted as a trigger to develop a child's thinking a stage further. Indeed, it became increasingly clear to me as the study progressed that discussing children's perceptions with them can play a vital role in their developing understanding.

This understanding rests, of course, on children's experience of literacy inside and outside the nursery. Fadua has watched her sister follow lines of print with her finger, Michelle enjoys the sense of security and peace when her mother reads silently, and Sade and Oleuwaseun have seen their parents reading and studying at home. The influence of these models is apparent in the children's behaviour and comments.

One child who expressed disgust at the sight of an adult novel may have a relative with literacy difficulties. Understanding that reading is not an exclusively oral activity is an important development in children who are not yet reading as Ferreiro and Teberosky (1982: 159) have pointed out, and Sade and Oleuwaseun's observations have helped them to achieve this understanding.

Children watch adults and older siblings reading in order to be able to imitate their reading behaviours. They will inevitably see adults engaged in functional reading – shopping lists, street signs, adverts on television, and so on, but they also need to observe sustained silent reading, the recreational or purposeful reading represented in the home by the variety of newspapers, magazines, pamphlets and books. To extend this experience into the nursery is difficult because of lack of time, yet there is no reason why adults working in the nursery should not take along their personal reading material to show children and talk about the pleasure and purposes of reading in their own lives. Talking generally about reading, and about the models children have seen, can only serve to further their understanding of the reading process.

Thanks to the explosion of research into early literacy development, we now appreciate the active nature of children's developing understanding of the reading process and the importance of encouraging reflection on language and how it works. Jeni Riley cites an increase in children's increasing explicit knowledge about language as literacy develops, both at surface and deep structural levels (2006: 41). Moreover, children engage in metacognitive activity when they attempt to solve the puzzles posed by the conversion of marks on the page into meaningful language. Yetta Goodman (1984: 102) reminded us over 20 years ago that children's thinking on this process constantly changes: 'children discover and invent literacy as they participate actively in a literate society'.

And, as Gunther Kress (2004: 75) asserts, 'each child finds her own path to literacy'. Children construct principles based on individual observations – for example, that speaking out loud is essential to reading, that 'looking' is important in silent reading, or that you have to follow lines of print with your finger to read. We need to be aware of these developments and to encourage discussion and reflection on the reading process so that principles which are not productive can be discarded.

It is surely an important part of our role as teachers of reading to encourage discussion and reflection when children do voice their developing understanding or indeed their confusion. Yassin's chance remark: 'How come you know the story?' made when I was reading a familiar book, would have provided a good opening for discussion, and Fadua's notion of the importance of the finger began to change as I talked to her. Children have a great deal to learn about reading, and their thoughts on the processes involved are fluid and changing. Their perceptions and attitudes by the age of 3 or 4 will influence their future development as readers and indeed as writers and talkers. All adults working with children have an important part to play in fostering children's confidence as readers and encouraging them to reflect on what it is they have to do to become readers in the fullest sense. Understanding how silent reading works and the pleasure that an adult experiences when absorbed in a book or magazine is a vital stage in this development. The complexities of the relationship between reader and print continue to tax the best adult minds – children need all the help they can get.

Acknowledgement

With thanks to the children and staff at Ainsworth Nursery.

References

Ferreiro, E. and Teberosky, A. (1982) *Literacy Before Schooling*, Oxford: Heinemann Educational.
Garner, A. (1980) Interview, in N. Chambers (ed.) *The Signal Approach to Children's Books*, Woodchester: Thimble Press.
Goodman, Y. (1984) 'The development of initial literacy', in Hillel Goelman et al. (eds) *Awakening to Literacy*, Oxford: Heinemann Educational.
Hall, N. (1987) *The Emergence of Literacy*, London: Hodder and Stoughton.
Kress, Gunther (2004) '"You make it like a crocodile" A theory of children's meaning-making', in T. Grainger (ed.) *Reader in Language and Literacy*, London: RoutledgeFalmer.
Riley, Jeni (2006) *Language and Literacy 3–7*, London: Sage.
Sartre, J.-P. (1964) *Les Mots*, Paris: Editions Gallimard.

In this chapter we encountered very young children constructing their own theories about what happens when adults say they are reading but children can see and hear no evidence of this. I love the way Sade believes that silent reading involves going 'dm dm dm' inside the brain and Joshua talks about the 'stick' Gillian has in her head which goes down her trousers and into her shoes. All of this is rich evidence of how hard young children work to make sense of the world, including the extremely confusing aspects of the world like reading silently.

Chapter 21

Hannah and her books

Sandra Smidt

Babies need books. No one would argue with that nowadays. One has only to look in bookshops to see how many books are being produced specifically for babies to see how a potential market has been exploited. One has only to talk to parents who have been involved in some of the 'books for babies' projects to appreciate how true this is. But what do babies get from books? Why are books important not only in the early years, but in the early months?

In this chapter, we look at how one baby, growing up in a house full of books, interacts with books and try and explore what it is she is learning from this experience. Hannah is almost 10 months old. She crawls, pulls herself upright, babbles to herself as she explores her world, climbs up on her mum's knee for a cuddle and greets each new day and situation as something to be explored and enjoyed. Like other babies of her age she is intensely interested in everything and will spend considerable amounts of time exploring new objects and achieving goals she sets herself. As an only child she has the benefit of a great deal of adult love and attention. She also has the advantage of having been introduced to stories, rhymes, songs and books from birth.

Her books include board books, waterproof books, hardback and paperback books. She has flap books, books with photographs of babies like herself, counting books and story books. We examine how Hannah interacts with the books and with the adults around the books to try and understand what she is interested in and how this helps her understand her world.

What is this thing and how does it work?

Hannah sees people around her reading books, papers and newspapers. She also sees people holding the books they read aloud to her, turning the pages and often pointing to words or pictures on the page.

When she was $9\frac{1}{2}$ months old, her mother reported that she had spent something like two hours exploring her box of books. With her back turned to her mother, Sam – who was sitting at the opposite end of the room – she spent the time taking the books out of the box, choosing some to pore over and rejecting others. Her exploration of the books seemed to relate to turning them over and over, sometimes holding them upwards, exploring the pictures and print on the cover, paying great attention to some picture or pattern. At first Sam thought she was selecting the books she knew well for further exploration, but it emerged that this was not the case. Her selection of books appeared random – although it almost certainly wasn't. But quite why Hannah rejected some of the books remained unclear.

A few days later (and after more similar play with the books) Hannah was seen sitting upright on the floor and holding a book just as she had seen adults do. She tends now to get the books the right way up and to start from the front and move to the back. She peers at the pictures and turns the pages with skill and care.

We guessed – and it can be no more than that – that her exploration of the books had helped her sort out the orientation of the books and to achieve her goal of holding a book 'like a reader'.

Pictures and naming

Like most young children, Hannah's life is bathed in language. Those who care for her talk through the routines of bath time and nappy changing; they sing her songs and chant rhymes; they play finger games and peekaboo. Embedded in this sea of words Hannah finds meaning by tuning into individual words or phrases which she now recognises, and which are always set in meaningful contexts. Like all babies Hannah uses the context to get at the meaning. Her recognition of individual words and phrases has led her to the point of 'requesting' names for things she is interested in. She makes her meaning clear by pointing, eye pointing and vocalising.

When she looks at her books she makes little noises to indicate recognition. When she sees a picture of a cat, for example, she makes a sound – looks at the adult, who almost invariably scaffolds her learning by saying something like 'Yes, it's a cat, isn't it?' – and beams. It is easy to understand this naming when it relates to the real objects in her world – things like a cat or a baby or a flower. But she also demands the naming of things which are totally 'unreal' to her. *Rosie's Walk* by Pat Hutchins (1968) is full of things Hannah has never seen or experienced. She has no knowledge of foxes or hens or goats, yet she requests the naming of these creatures and will then select one for special attention. She will leaf through the pages of the book until she comes to the page she wants (most often the one showing the goat) and study the picture with intense concentration as she plays her 'name it for me' game.

As Hannah encounters images in books she is able to discover that not all cats look exactly like her cat: yet they are still cats. She is beginning to classify. Very recently Hannah came upon the picture of the camel in *Dear Zoo* (Campbell 1982). Her grandmother said, 'It's a camel – and look, Hannah, here's another camel', and showed her a picture of a camel in *Where's Julius?* (Burningham 1988) and then a drawing of a camel on a cigarette package and a stuffed camel made by a child in Egypt. Hannah looked carefully from one to another: one would guess she was trying to find what features made all four images share the label 'camel'.

When Hannah was a small baby her parents bought her a set of books based on a theory (popular at that time) that young babies respond to high contrast images. She did pay some attention to these black and white images, but showed no preference for them over other images she was introduced to. From the age of about three months she showed intense interest in paintings and objects in her environment. The pictures she encounters in books clearly also interest her and for a long time she seemed very tuned in to images on a dark background – the cat on the wall against the night sky in *Peace at Last* (Murphy 1992) and the animals going home in the dark in *Where Does Brown Bear Go?* (Weiss 1989). She demonstrates her interest in these pictures by paying prolonged attention to them and requesting names for the images she focuses on.

Browne (1994) found that her daughter Rehana was interested in complex, bright pictures until the age of six months, but then, for a short while, preferred simpler images. Hannah shows evidence of this by the intense concentration she lavishes on pictures both in books and on the walls. At the moment she demands to be shown two Chagall prints which are complex, colourful and full of movement. So she will now point to 'the sun playing the violin' or 'the red horse with a fish and a bird in its head'. It is fascinating to speculate on what sense Hannah is able to make of such eye-catching images, representing things fantastical and way beyond her experience.

Books as toys

Hannah uses books for different purposes. She now, at the age of 10 months, is very used to flap books and is able to turn down the flaps with great dexterity. Her favourite of these is *How Many Bugs in the Box?* (Carter 1992). For a long time she wanted to interact physically with the book, turning down the flaps, opening them and showing glee when the 'bugs' were revealed, but when she reached the page where the seven space bugs have to be revealed by grasping a small piece of ribbon and lifting it, she sat back and waited for the adult to do this. After several weeks of watching closely exactly how this was done, she suddenly pushed my hand out of the way, grasped the ribbon very deliberately and accurately and lifted the flap. Her delight was palpable.

Often, in books, she is looking for and at human faces. Her interest in photographs of people she recognises has been apparent from when she was very small and to capitalise on that she has been given a specially made photograph album containing pictures of herself and her family and friends (rather like Jessica's[1] scrap book). She will spend a long time smiling with recognition and turning the pages to find a particular photograph. One has the caption 'Hannah's got a serious face' and when she reaches that page she always looks up at the adult and composes her normally smiling features into a 'serious' expression!

The power of stories

Hannah has had stories told and read to her from when she was very tiny. At first she would glance at the pictures and respond to the sound of the human voice reading aloud. But her interest and attention were limited. Gradually, however, she has begun to not only enjoy hearing stories read and told, but has begun to 'demand' them. She now adopts a particular position – leaning back against the adult reader in a position of great warmth and comfort. She listens raptly to the words and pays great attention to the stories. At ten months she can listen to stories with extended texts – such as *So Much* by Trish Clark, *Peace at Last* by Jill Murphy (1992) and *Where the Wild Things Are* by Maurice Sendak (1964). She will listen to each of these from beginning to end, held snugly against the adult and focused on the pictures.

What can such a young child be getting from this experience? The meaning cannot possibly be central to her since the books explore ideas and concepts way beyond Hannah's experience. She is interested in the pictures and pays attention to these as the story is read. It is clearly a very warm and loving experience – held close to an adult, having that adult's undivided attention, adult and child focused on the same thing and bathed in language. But there seems to be more to it than that. There is something about the very language of the books, the themes they explore and the complex and vivid illustrations that captures and holds Hannah's interest. Each of these books is very different and it is worth trying to examine what it might be that Hannah gains from each of these.

Where the Wild Things Are (Sendak 1964) was perhaps the first story book Hannah had read to her. She would listen to the words and sometimes glance at the pictures and if someone recited the text of the book to her without showing her the book she listened with complete absorption. She clearly doesn't know what wild things are, what it means to feel lonely or understand how to work through anger and fear. There is something about the very language of the book – something about the rhythm and lilt of the words – that means something to such a young child. Maurice Sendak in using such poetic language has clearly tuned into one of the things that young children attend to. In addition, the sensitive and complex illustrations – very unlike the oversimplified images often encountered in books for babies – engage Hannah's attention for long periods of time.

Peace at Last (Murphy 1992) was first read to Hannah at about the same time that she began to crawl and to encounter the word 'no'. Her mobility brought her into situations that were potentially dangerous and her parents started using the word 'no' and shaking their heads. Hannah quickly imitated the shaking of the head and did it every time she heard the word 'no', whatever the context. So when she listened to *Peace at Last* (Murphy 1992), every time the reader got to the refrain '"Oh, no" said Mr Bear', Hannah would frantically shake her head and grin. In this book she is particularly tuned in to the sounds represented in the book and to the repeated patterns of language. She was given a miniature version of the book and her first response was to throw it away in disgust. When it was then read to her she kept her eyes fixed on the reader's face with an expression of disbelief on her face. When she was then shown the large and small versions of the book at the same time and shown that they are identical in everything but size, she was extremely interested.

So Much! (Cooke 1994) is about a black baby celebrating a birthday party with his family. The illustrations are graphic and sensitive and the language – like that of the

Sendak book – is poetic and rhythmic with the added feature that it is in dialect. The book is full of features designed to attract a small child. On each page we encounter the baby waiting with his mum for a ring at the doorbell and the entry of a family member. The text ends with 'It was …' encouraging prediction and the build-up of anticipation. Hannah has had a lot of experience of predicting what will happen next. Some of this comes from her knowledge of rhymes and games and finger plays: some from the rough and tumble games she plays with her dad; and some from her experience of flap books. In this book each family member wants to show their love for the baby in some way – by kissing or squeezing or fighting the baby. Hannah waits for these moments of physical interaction with the reader and shows her enthusiasm by kissing and squeezing back.

Hannah will listen to each of these stories and at the end demand a repetition. She is able to sustain her interest and attention over a long period of time.

What this tells us about emergent readers

Like many children, Hannah's first exposure to literacy has been within her home and family. The literature activities she gets involved in are set in the context of all of Hannah's activities – playing with everything she encounters in order to understand the world she inhabits. Her parents and the other adults she encounters around these literacy events are all following Hannah's lead. They allow her to select the literacy activity (does she want to be read to or to explore the books?) and follow her lead – sometimes leaving her to explore, other times naming things for her and often reading the stories she has selected. In this reading of stories, Hannah is not a passive recipient. She indicates by her pointing, her vocalising and her body language, the features of the story or pictures which interest her. There have been many studies of young children's responses to stories and books: most of them focus on the years when children begin to respond verbally. Although we can have no definitive answer to what is going on in a young child's mind, the physical evidence of total involvement in the world of books is persuasive. Hannah will spend prolonged periods of time physically exploring books with her hands and with her eyes: she will watch with enormous concentration what the adults do with books and then imitate these actions, spending time on perfecting her physical skills: she will get deeply engrossed in the pictures and shapes on the page and will, again, spend time searching for something she particularly wants to see: she adopts a particular physical stance when she wants to listen to a story and remains alert, attentive and responsive throughout these reading sessions. No one who has met Hannah has any doubt that she will acquire language and begin talking. She will not need lessons in how to talk. As she engages with print and fantasy through her play and exploration and is able to watch competent readers reading, she is developing a positive orientation to literacy. She expects books to be interesting, exciting, fun and comforting. It is more than tempting to suggest that if she is allowed to play with books and languages in this way she will become a reader, just like Jessie.[1] Watch this space!

A year on

Hannah is now 22 months old. She is talking non-stop, combining words into sentences and showing, in her wide vocabulary, how much of her learning about the world and about language itself has come from books. She now acts like a reader, sometimes 'reading' the books to her teddies who are required to sit on her lap and 'listen to the 'tory'. Often she retells stories with remarkable accuracy, remembering the sequence of events and turning pages with agility. If she, by mistake, turns over two pages at once, she reminds herself 'one at a time'.

She was given a set of magnetic letters and told the names of the ones she showed interest in. Now she not only pays attention to the pictures, but often, also to the print. She will point to letters she knows and comment 'S for Sana, H for Hannah, M for mummy', and so on. She notices the difference between capital and lower-case letters – as when she commented, when finding an 'h', 'Oh, a baby h for Hannah'. (Since the birth of her baby brother, Ben, all large objects are classified as 'mummy' and all small objects as 'baby'!)

Hannah is also beginning to understand some of the different forms and purposes of writing. Stories retold by her often start with 'wunsaponatime', but a letter or a card is read as 'Dear mummy, mmmmmmm, love from Hannah'.

Hannah's ability to make links between fantasy and reality is fascinating. When listening to a story she will rush off, in the middle, to fetch things from her real life that appear in the book – a teddy, when she listens to *Peace at Last* (Murphy 1992) or an animal that occurs in *Bringing the Rain to Kapiti Plain* (Aardemam 1981) or *The Honey Hunters* (Martin 1994). She also now comments on things she remembers from the stories – saying 'in the book' – making clear that she is able to distinguish reality from fantasy.

A new book is viewed with excitement and some uncertainty. She demands to hear it again and again before she will attempt to join in or spend time looking through it on her own. Words are her passion and, as with a book or story that is new, a new word has to be repeated and repeated until Hannah with astounding understanding uses the new word in a different context – but always preserving the meaning.

And today

Hannah is now 13 years old – a teenager, but still an involved, critical and serious reader. She learned to 'lift the tune from the page' (to use Myra Barr's phrase) with ease but her experience at primary school did not make her into a writer. All the 'writing' time at school was spent on things like drafting a story, plotting the sequence of events, describing a character and so on. No opportunities for extended writing for an audience. So Hannah only became a writer when she went to secondary school and met a soulmate and the two started to write long, complex and shared stories. When Hannah was invited to contribute some of her writing to this book she wanted, at first to use some of this shared writing, but this never happened.

Instead, some months ago, just after a death in her family, we were at the theatre waiting for a play to start when Hannah asked if anyone had some paper because she wanted to write down a poem she had in her head. Between us, all we could find were two supermarket receipts. It was on these that Hannah wrote down the first draft of the poem that follows. Hannah gave it no title.

Note

1 Refers to Jessica in Chapter 23 by Evelyn Slavid.

References

Aardemam, V. (1981) *Bringing the Rain to Kapiti Plain*, London: Macmillan Children's Books.
Browne, N. (1994) 'I'm Three Years Old and I Can Read', *GAEC Newsletter* No 6.
Burningham, J. (1988) *Where's Julius?*, London: Picture Piper.
Campbell, R. (1982) *Dear Zoo*, London: Picture Puffin.
Carter, D. (1992) *How Many Bugs in the Box?*, London: Orchard Books.
Cooke, T. (1994) *So Much!*, London: Walker Books.
Hall, N. (1987) *The Emergence of Literacy*, London: Hodder and Stoughton.
Hutchins, P. (1968) *Rosie's Walk*, London: Picture Puffin.
Martin, F. (1994) *The Honey Hunters*, London: Walker Books.
Meek, M. (1991) *On Being Literate*, London: Bodley Head.
Murphy, J. (1992) *Peace at Last*, London: Picture Mac.
Sendak, M. (1964) *Where the Wild Things Are*, London: Bodley Head.
Weiss, N. (1989) *Where Does Brown Bear Go?* London: Picture Puffin.

Chapter 22

A Poem

Hannah Gardiner

Here at last!' my voice does cry,
And I spread my coal-black wings and fly,
Into the sun-drenched fields of rye
That do make up my home
The caws of ravens, magpies, crows,
In the crops all sown in long, straight rows,
And the fields all ploughed by a thousand hoes
That welcome me back home.
And I land on quiet, unsure feet,
See how fast my Heart does beat,
As I scan the patch of brazen wheat
That used to be my home.
But I see no sign of loved ones here,
No trace of feather, fur or hair,
And I hear the neigh of a stricken mare
On the borders of my home.
And understanding strikes me cruelly,
As now I realise that, truly,
Through the blazing haze of fury,
Their lives are at an end.
Again I spread these glossy wings,
To fly on to better things.
And though the pain of death still stings,
This is no more my home.
And as I soar into the sky,
A bang does overcome my cry,
But as I try to rise up high,
I find I cannot move.
The bullet's aim is straight and true,
Straight into my breast it flew,
And I realise that my life, too,
Is coming to an end.
I spin and fall through clear skies,
Though no sight meets my glassy eyes,

As my poor heart stutters and fails and tries
To save my worthless life.
But my body feels no more pain,
As my red blood soaks the earth like rain,
And my life is left to rot and decay,
A scavenger, nothing more.
The humans do not look for me,
My broken body is left to bleed,
They do not regret this wicked deed
On the land I once called home.
And flowers bloom before my eyes,
And though I know they are nought but lies,
I cannot help but weep inside.
I have died at home.

Reading this, it is easy to spot the influence of literature and the power of words and music for Hannah. She can now compose her own tunes and inscribe them on the page.

Chapter 23

Learning to read made easy

A study of one child's development as a reader

Evelyn Slavid

Evelyn Slavid has been involved in education for many years – in schools and beyond. This chapter appeared in the first edition.

Jessica is 5 years, 10 months old. I have just tested her reading age using a test called 'New Reading Analysis' (NFER Nelson) and found that her reading score comes out at about age 11 and her comprehension age at the same. I do not hold great store by tests like these and the fact that I administered the test myself could, of course, be open to criticism. However, Jessica spends a lot of time reading and really enjoys it. I was interested to see if this was reflected in the test score.

If I examine her favourite books at present, I discover that they are quite diverse: Enid Blyton adventure stories, 'Milly Molly Mandy' stories and lots of poetry including works by Michael Rosen and Brian Patten. I have never stopped her from reading anything she has been given or chosen, but will always talk to her about the stereotypes some authors display. She is, I feel, learning to be critical about the books she reads. She often chooses to read books with her friends. They take turns to read stories to each other. She also swaps books and they often talk to one another about what they are reading. So reading, for Jess, is not just a solitary activity, but a social one as well. Jessica has just passed through a stage where she would read stories but not in the order in which they were written. I found this very strange and when I asked her why she did this she said that certain chapters sounded more interesting than others and so she read those chapters first. I then asked her if she thought that the author would mind, but she said no, because she read the whole book in the end. It was fascinating for me to hear the author P.D. James talking about how she writes her books and to hear that she doesn't write them sequentially, but starts with the scenes or actions that interest her most at the time. So maybe Jessica is onto something!

When I was asked to write about Jessica's reading development, I didn't know where to start. As a working mother I felt that I hadn't done anything different from any other parent. But when I observed other parents and thought about how much I had learnt as a teacher, I realised that, when it came to teaching my own child to read, I possessed knowledge that other parents may not have had access to. I was lucky in that I was teaching at a time when reading schemes were being removed from the school I worked in to be replaced by 'real books' and when Waterland (1985) and Bennett (1979) were compulsory reading for primary teachers. It was also a time when reading was regarded as a developmental process along with walking and talking. Armed with this information I then became a parent. I did not find parenting in general an easy process and found I did not have a great deal of time to observe my child's progress. Many friends suggested I should keep diaries of her progress. I never managed this in any detail, although I wrote down certain milestones.

What I did do with Jessica was to talk to her about print. We would look at the writing on things like cereal boxes, etc. I provided her with lots of books – plastic books and material books, but mostly picture books which might have been deemed more suitable for older children (mostly hand-downs from friends). She had an alphabet frieze in her room. But the most important thing we did was to read to her as often as possible from when she was about 9 months old. When she first started speaking I played games with her using books, e.g. showing her a picture with a word underneath, covering up the word and saying, 'What do you think the word says?' I would then uncover the word and we would both be pleased that she had, of course, guessed the correct word. All that this game did was to draw her attention to print. It was fun – and it distinguished between picture and word. I have to emphasise that I would never suggest covering up the pictures and expecting the child to read the words. The important thing about it was that it was in the context of a game which Jessica enjoyed and in which success was guaranteed.

Another thing I did at this very early stage was to make Jessica a book about herself. I would love to be able to say that this was a well-produced and finished item. In reality it was a scrap book where I stuck odd photographs of Jessica and her friends and family and wrote simple, descriptive sentences, e.g. 'Jess is pointing at her dad' or 'Where is Jessica's mum?' She loved to 'read' this book and learnt it off by heart and would want to 'read' it to other people. It was during this 'reading' that I observed interesting comments from some friends and family. They would actually say, 'She's not reading. She knows it off by heart'. This seemed a strange reaction from people who happily interpret the most unintelligible utterances as 'words' and the first hesitant steps usually ending up as a tumble, as 'walking'. This book is still a favourite of Jessica's and she still enjoys showing it to friends and family. What I also did with this book was to sometimes point to words on the page, such as 'I' and say 'Can you see that it's the same here?' (pointing to another 'I'). This helped Jessica realise that the same symbol or set of symbols always says the same thing.

Before she could read I never tried to teach Jessica the sounds that letters make, but she learnt the alphabet by singing songs. It was only once she started reading that we talked specifically about the sounds that letters make.

It was coincidental that I became aware that Jess actually realised print–word correspondence because, when she was about 19 months old, she was videoed by a relative. He later sent me a copy and in this video Jess can be clearly seen pointing to the word 'I' and then pointing to her own eye and saying 'I'. Now there is clearly some confusion for her about meaning, but, at this very early age, she was able to identify a symbol as having a meaning of some sort.

Some of Jessica's favourite books were those where she could join in and make noises or help by finding things in the pictures. She often wanted to 'read' the story to me, which was great, and, although she was really telling me the story, I would once or twice draw her attention to print by saying things like, 'Can you see a word that starts with the same letter/sound as your name?' I need to stress that I would not interrupt the flow of the story, but wait until the end before doing this.

I continued reading stories to Jessica – interesting picture books and sometimes the same book night after night after night she usually chose, although sometimes, in desperation, I would hide the book that had gone on for too long and introduce something different. As Jess got older, she would talk about the picture more and more and recognise more words. It was at this later stage that I started talking to her about the sounds that different letters make. I always used the name and the sound of the letter as I believe that even at an early stage children are able to understand that this, for example, is the letter 'A' and it usually makes the sound 'a' as in 'apple'.

One of the other special things that has happened for Jessica is that, from when she was very young, her father has made up stories for her. They started when she was about 2 years old and involve the same core characters, with additional characters brought in from time to time by Jessica or by Peter (her father). I see them as a sort of soap opera! Many different issues are dealt with in these stories (known as the 'Emma' stories). Even though the core characters remain the same, it was only last week that I discovered that one of them was blind. Jessica has always loved the 'Emma' stories and, if given the choice of being read a story or told a story, it will be told a story every time. Jess has learnt a great deal of what she knows through these stories – about plants, animals, love, jealousy. There is so much that children can learn through the medium of stories.

When Jess went to a childminder I was adamant that I did not want her to be taught to read, and it was the same when she went to nursery. The childminder read her lots of stories and sang rhymes to her and when she went to a nursery they read a wide selection of stories. They did many activities based on nursery rhymes, sang songs and used many aids and props while telling stories. It was a nursery that did not teach children to read, although many nurseries in the area pride themselves on the fact that they do!

When it came to choosing a school for Jess, I was determined that we needed to choose a school where she would not be put off reading. I visited many schools and was shocked by the number that insisted that children work their way through a reading scheme, regardless of ability or interest. I was amazed when one parent at a local playgroup where I was giving a talk on early reading, expounded the virtues of a school where her child had read 120 books in the same reading scheme. I felt so sorry for the child! I eventually found a school where, although they used reading scheme books, they allowed children to choose what they wanted to read from a wide selection of books. The school provides an atmosphere in which reading is valued. All the children (aged 4–11) have a quiet reading time during the day. Fiction and non-fiction books are present in all the classrooms and are easily accessible to the children.

More recently I have turned my attention to the way that Jessica's enjoyment of stories has carried over into her writing. I was, originally, very sceptical about emergent/developmental writing. But I now realise how it gives children the freedom and confidence to write. Jessica and her friends, both at home and in school, often choose to write and make up stories for and about each other. I believe that this is due to the fact that, at school, they have been given the chance to be successful writers (in terms of composition), without fear of being criticised for incorrect spellings. The stories Jess writes are often based on the stories she has read or been told. She knows how to get help with spelling, but for her, the essential bit of writing – the meaning of her stories – is allowed to develop.

I want to conclude by saying that I don't feel that anything I have done has been difficult. Jessica says she doesn't remember how she learnt to read, although she does remember one or two favourite books (like *The Very Hungry Caterpillar*) that she spent time looking at when she was little. She says that she learnt those books off by heart – and was then able to read. This is, of course, an oversimplification of a complex process. But learning to read was easy for Jess – maybe because it was pressure-free, fun and because she always understood the purpose of reading and the pleasures to be found in books.

References

Bennett, J. (1979) *Learning to Read with Picture Books*, Woodchester: Thimble Press.
Waterland, L. (1985) *Read with Me – An Apprenticeship Approach to Reading*, Woodchester: Thimble Press.

When this chapter was written, Jess was 5 years old. She is now an adult and a medical student and when she was asked if she would like to write a response to it, she did so. The next chapter is what she said.

Chapter 24

My life as a reader

Jess Slavid-Buckle

I was fascinated to read my mum's account of the way in which I became a reader. I still cannot remember learning to read. I think that this is probably because, for me, reading was never a 'chore'. However, the presence of stories, storytelling, poetry and song are extremely prevalent among my childhood memories. I was lucky enough not to be made to undergo any 'formulaic' processes such as reading schemes or phonetics lessons. I was never criticised for getting something wrong. I was never 'forced' to read anything I didn't want to. Instead, it was a cycle of immersion, choice, enjoyment and encouragement, which opened up a new, exciting world of creativity and fun. In this way, I can honestly say that, for me, reading was merely an extension of 'play'. I can remember a friend of mine telling me, when she was about 8, that she was not a 'free' reader. At the time my mother asked her why, and she said that in her school she was not free to choose what she read or how she read. Looking back, this strikes me as a clear contrast between my early experiences of reading, and those of many other children. I have since found out that the (highly prestigious) school, at which this friend was a student, boasted to parents that 'many of the children had reading ages of 12, by the time they were in Year 2'!

I am in fact, quite sceptical about what 'reading ages' really mean. My mother has written about how, aged 5, I had a 'reading age' of 11. However, I found the transition from the 'child and teenage' part of Waterstone's bookshop to the 'adult' section to be surprisingly painful. Looking at my bookshelf, I can still see many Jacqueline Wilson books, a few Roald Dahl novels and a wide selection of children's poetry. I would be lying if I said that I did not flick through these from time to time. Therefore, although I am now 19, in some ways, my 'reading age' clearly has not changed!

I actually think that it is important to recognise that, even at my age, I am still 'learning to read' and need advice and encouragement. I continue to love reading and the insights into life that I constantly gain from books (e.g. *The Kite Runner, My Sister's Keeper* and *The Curious Incident of the Dog in the Night-time*). However, moving to secondary school, I was overwhelmed by the vast array of exams, social events and extra-curricular activities. Unlike my primary school, there was no 'book corner', 'silent reading time' or 'class story-time'. I was being persuaded by my parents and teachers to start reading 'adult' books, yet I did not enjoy these as much. In addition, as SATs, GCSE and A-level English assessments approached, the 'free' and 'relaxing' aspects of reading seemed virtually diminished. While I continued to read when I had a chance, many of my friends did not and would actively dismiss reading. I am now at university, and do not read (for enjoyment) as much as I would like to.

I therefore think that schools and the media could do much more to help students discover what books they enjoy, and encourage reading for pleasure. For example, I recently chose to study a poetry module as part of my medical degree. I really enjoyed exploring science and art in such close proximity and found that reading and writing poetry was a surprisingly fun way of broadening my perspectives on many levels, medical and non-medical. Interestingly, the innovatively artistic nature of this module reminded me partly of my English lessons in my primary school and I was delighted to rediscover the joy of creative reading and writing. Therefore, while the attractions offered by television, the Internet, and social activities continue to escalate; it does not surprise me that fewer teenagers are reading for fun. Perhaps if more young people were given opportunities like the one I have just described, where the principles of learning rely upon exploring literature freely and imaginatively, this may help to prevent them and others from being 'put off' reading.

Part VI

Representing thoughts and feelings

In recent years there has been little emphasis on the creative aspects of learning which has meant that children have developed a sense that things like painting and drawing and music and dance and drama are not important. Clearly this is not so and finding ways to allow children to express their thoughts and feelings in as many ways as possible is gradually creeping back into the curriculum. In this part, we look at three ways of representing feelings and ideas – drawing/painting, making and music. For the first time we move away from a focus on the youngest children and start to look at an extraordinary 'experiment' which took place in post-apartheid South Africa when a British viola player became involved in a project introducing classical music and the discipline required to make it within a group of others to children who had previously had no experience of either the music or the discipline. Rosemary Nalden's work is becoming known throughout the world and I am extremely grateful to her for writing the key chapter which closes this part and leads perfectly into the last part of the book.

Chapter 25

Scaffolding Caitlin's learning

Emma Stoddart

Emma Stoddart was a student on the Early Childhood Studies Scheme. Here she explores in detail what she learned as she watched Caitlin draw. Caitlin was 2 years, 11 months old at the time and Emma was particularly interested in Caitlin's thoughts and ideas and feelings and also in the influence the adult had in this situation.

As an early-years worker and an adult who considers myself unable to draw, I am interested in how young children, making marks, are influenced by the adults around them. How can the attitudes and responses of these adults support them in positive ways and what has gone wrong when a child gives up painting and drawing and grows up to believe that she 'cannot draw'? In this chapter, I wish to explore how a child can be offered an environment rich with opportunities to encourage her to make marks. I will do this by examining my observations of one child making marks and by evaluating my responses to her actions in the light of relevant research. I will define making marks as drawing or any other action which leaves a visible mark on a material. All children have a compulsion to make marks; whatever their culture they have a desire to leave a record, whether it be with crayons on paper, with a stick in the earth or with any other materials available to them. Making visual representations in this way is vital to a young child's development, both as a means of self-expression and because experience of symbolic representation is needed by the child as she actively tries to make sense of the world around her. We live in a symbolic world in which abstract symbolic representation in the form of written, spoken and sign language are central to our communication with each other.

Piaget suggested that children learn from their environment without interaction with adults or other children; he suggested that making marks starts with random scribbling, developing into intentional drawing only when an accidental mark, recognised as being a representation of a familiar object, is then repeated. By contrast, Matthews (1994) proposed that children make intentional marks right from the start to represent shape, movement and emotion in a way that is meaningful for them. By focusing on the child's process of mark-making rather than the end-product, adults can interact with the child in a way that is sensitive and supportive.

Indeed, this interaction is not only possible, but essential if the child's mark-making is to thrive.

I chose to observe Caitlin because I find her evident enjoyment of making marks very exciting. The observation took place in the playgroup in which I work. On this particular morning, I had provided felt tips, biros and coloured A4 paper on a small table. I had also put out carbon paper for the first time because I wished to offer the children a new material to explore. Other graphic materials, clearly labelled and within reach, were available to the children.

When Caitlin first begins to make marks on her chosen piece of paper, I sit beside her attending to what she is doing attentively, but in silence. I do not ask her what she is drawing, even when the image emerging on the paper starts, as I guess, to resemble the face and body of something or someone. At a certain point in her draw-ing, she offers me the information herself, commenting first 'A head!' and then, after further development of the image, 'A monster!' Thus my initial interaction with Caitlin supports Schirrmacher (1988), who suggests that when we notice a child's drawing we do not give our opinion of it immediately; rather, we should pause before we speak, to give ourselves space to think of an appropriate comment and the child space to voluntarily offer us information or start a discussion herself if she wishes.

As Caitlin draws (see Figure 25.1), she makes an enclosed shape by placing a base-line across the open end of an inverted U-shape; thus she represents the monster's body, a physical entity separate from the space on the rest of the paper.

She adds features to further define the head and body; she draws two parallel lines and a further two lines travelling down from the baseline to form two V marks; she then draws a single vertical line on each side of the monster's body, parallel to, but

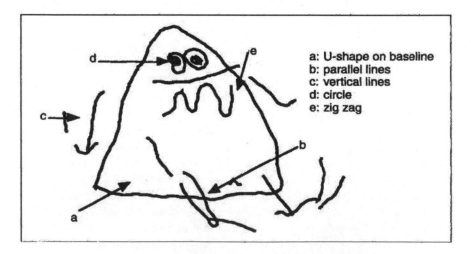

Figure 25.1 Caitlin's first drawing which she called 'a monster'

not touching it. I guess that these lines represent the monster's limbs and that the circles at the top of the head represent eyes, but since I do not ask Caitlin I cannot assume this. If I were to comment 'I see you are drawing some lines down from your monster's body' or 'Look, you've drawn two circles in the monster's head', I would indicate my interest in the added features without imposing my guesses on her, and she might well offer me more information.

To use the terms of Matthews (1994), Caitlin demonstrates in her first drawing that she can intentionally use a 'U-shape on a baseline', 'zigzags' and vertical lines. She can distinguish between the physical movements required of her to produce each different shape. She has drawn these shapes from her mark-making vocabulary and combined them in a way that is meaningful to her, to represent her monster in two-dimensional form.

When she starts to draw on her second piece of paper (Figure 25.2), she demonstrates additional marks in her vocabulary: 'waves' and 'variations on right angular joints'.

Finally, on the carbon paper (Figure 25.3) she makes a 'loop', a 'travelling zigzag' and, by 'continuous rotation', forms more closed shapes.

Throughout the observation I give Caitlin little feedback about what she is actually doing. Had I talked to her using informative language, scaffolding her progress (Bruner 1980) with comments on her zigzags, closed shapes and other marks, I could possibly have helped her to become more aware of how her representations were working. She, however, spontaneously offers me information from time to time.

By listening, I become aware of a sense of order among her marks and of her interest in forming letters, numbers and patterns. By tuning in to her processes, I become aware of her own vocabulary of marks, her mark-making schema, which I observe her repeating again and again.

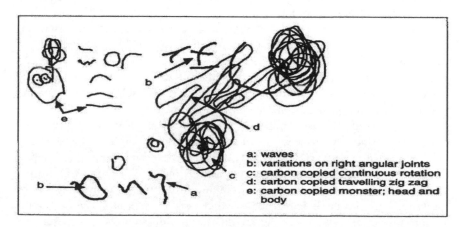

Figure 25.2 Caitlin's second drawing, in which the monster still features together with new marks and shapes

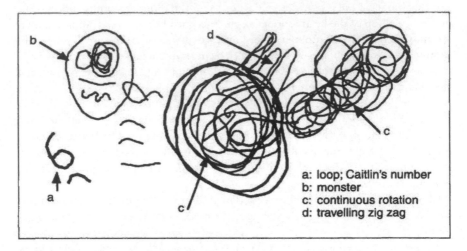

Figure 25.3 Caitlin's third drawing using carbon paper; the monster together
with numbers, a loop and zigzags

Throughout the observation, Caitlin demonstrates the ability to use both 'symbols' and 'signs' (Matthews 1994, after Piaget). Her representation of both of her monsters is symbolic, since she intends her images to reflect their actual physical appearance. By contrast, she is also concerned with signs, i.e. letters and numbers which are abstract representations. She shows this when she comments on her loop 'I did that number on mine' and 'I can do writing' as she proceeds to draw travelling zigzags. Although this latter zigzag is a sign, the zigzag on her first monster is probably part of its overall symbolic form. She is free-flowing (as Bruce 1991 might say) between making signs and symbols.

When Caitlin comes to use the carbon paper she is exploring a material that is new to her. I show her its duplicating property. When she asks for explanations, I try to use language which is accessible to her; she is, however, only partially able to grasp what I say. She needs time to explore what Hutt calls epistemic play in order to gain knowledge and skills of how carbon paper works. She is most likely to come to this understanding through hands-on experience at her own pace.

I plan to extend Caitlin's learning through mark-making from her present point of competence to a future point, i.e. through her zone of proximal development (Vygotsky 1978). Prentice (1994) points out that an adult can communicate support for a child's mark-making through both verbal and non-verbal responses. I can articulate my support to her verbally by continuing to use reflective listening and by speaking of my pleasure in her creations. My non-verbal support includes both my attention when she is mark-making, an indication of my interest, and the physical environment that I provide for her. I base my planning of the environment on her current interests and skills and decided to offer her a wide range of opportunities with different materials and tools, through which she can consolidate her present schemas and explore and develop them further.

References

Bruce, T. (1991) *Time to Play in Early Childhood*, London: Hodder and Stoughton.

Bruner, J. S. (1980) *Under Five in Britain* (Oxford Pre-School Research Project), Oxford: Grant McIntyre.

Matthews, J. (1994) *Helping Children to Draw and Paint in Early Childhood*, London: Hodder and Stoughton.

Prentice, R. (1994) 'Experimental learning in play and art', in J.R. Moyles (ed.) *The Excellence of Play*, Maidenhead: Open University Press.

Schirrmacher, R. (1988) *Art and Creative Development for Young Children*, New York: Van Nostrand Reinhold.

Vygotsky, L. S. (1978) *Mind in Society*, Cambridge, MA: Harvard University Press.

Chapter 26

The workshop table

A stepping stone in the visual arts

Duane Hernandez

Duane Hernandez, at the time of writing, was a teacher working in a nursery in East London and a student on the Nursery Certificate course at the University of North London – a course designed specifically to prepare teachers to teach young children. We have not been able to trace him to get his approval for including an edited version of his original in this edition.

The general approach to the visual arts within the nursery at which I work has been the main table 'art activity'. A special and quite expansive area is set aside for this and provision varies on a daily basis. Generally, the activities presented are based on the adults' ideas and assumptions and are adult-led. The dangers of this kind of approach are only too clear in the light of what is known about play and about the importance of adults following the interests of the child. The following observation highlights all my concerns:

> A vase containing daffodils has been presented to the children with the intention of a still-life study in either paint or collage materials – green and yellow only provided. On the main art activity table Yvonne, for the second time, has spread glue on the back of her card and stuck it to the newspaper on the table. This time round she is writing her name (all the letters perfectly), covering the whole A4 card presumably on what she considered to be the back to the tune of 'Oh Yvonne! You've stuck it to the table … Look, let me show you'. Yvonne, having heard the explanation from the adult now spreads glue all over her name and starts to stick scraps of materials (the colour of daffodils) on to her piece of A4 card.

Yvonne's main preoccupations were, in the first instance, simply spreading the glue – and, second, as evidenced from previous observations where she painted each letter of her name in huge letters at the easel on successive occasions, a celebration of writing her name. It is sad when adults cut across the child's potential for learning and expression like this. We are all guilty of this from time to time. The most worrying aspect is that some of us may not even be aware of it. We may ask what the consequences may be if we choose to ignore the child's central role in her/his learn-ing in the visual arts. I concur with Jameson (1974) in that children lose their 'spon-taneity' and 'motivation' and may well become dependent on direction by the adult. This is heightened in children of nursery age, who are powerless in comparison to adults and all too eager to please them.

The workshop table: A re-evaluation

The workshop table? This needs some explaining here. What used to be on offer in our nursery's creative areas were: sand, water, dough table, painting at the easel, graphics table and a main art activity table. Essentially, the bare bones of what might be called a workshop environment. Caught up within the main art activity provision was a whole host of experiences that needed fleshing out to produce a more worth-while environment for the children. The teacher before me had attempted to do this and failed and I was not confident of my ground here with regard to the other edu-cators in the nursery. I decided to create opportunities for writing/graphics in other contexts, e.g. developing space elsewhere and in context, for instance, within socio-dramatic play. I nevertheless held on to the graphics side of what was the graphics table, but developed its scope to become what I called the 'make and do' table. Here there were opportunities for the children to make three-dimensional creations, to cut and stick (with stickers), use hole punches, and so on. A fairly limited step in the differentiation and accessibility of activities usually associated with the main art activity. The children responded as expected, with enthusiasm. The adults went some way to accommodating success here.

However, at the start of the new academic year, we completely changed the nurs-ery, so that the creative area was now based in the other room. Nevertheless, I had managed to secure a shelved unit for the 'make and do' table, which, it was hoped, would create better opportunities for choice. Initially, things appeared to be work-ing well, but it was soon apparent that enthusiasm had begun to wane. On observ-ing the situation, I discovered that one of the reasons for this was that adults were pre-structuring the table. Materials and resources would be put out that the children did not necessarily feel inclined to use, e.g. chalks and chalkboards – and those who were committed had to proceed with such things in their way to achieve their goals. This was happening more and more, and, before Christmas I even found holly and red and green pens specifically selected for the purpose of making observational drawing.

To take stock of this situation, I decided to perform a little experiment. I sought the cooperation of the adults in the nursery and for 3 days, nothing was added to the table in this way. The children were free to select what they liked from the shelves – but few did. Those who did asked permission or were encouraged to do so as they approached the table. Hence, part of the reason for the table's demise was that the message children were getting was that adults selected the materials and resources and some children, understandably, came to depend on this. It took an interested adult to encourage and guide children in making choices and hence use the table again. The role of interested and engaged adults is crucial here as is it in almost all aspects of learning.

Finally the resourcing and presentation of the area needed sorting out. Things had landed up on the shelves that were of no real interest to the children – like leftovers from cut-out photographs. What the children needed were the materials and resources that really set the imagination going – things like wire paper ties. Also lacking was a suitable way of presenting three-dimensional 'junk' materials. A wheeled vegetable trolley was the solution. We also made sure that basic tools like scissors, stickers, hole punches, felt pens, and others were readily at hand.

The 'make and do' table lost its name and became the DIY (do it yourself) table. This embodied the new spirit, but ignored the important role of the adult. The scope of the table was limited, but the intention was always that it becomes a stepping stone towards a more diversified workshop environment.

The learning/creative process: What the children showed us

The most rewarding aspect of all this was that the workshop table took off very quickly and became a centre for a certain kind of creativity and learning. I would like to share some of this with the reader – looking particularly at autonomy, agendas, play, motivation, self-expression, technological thought, communication, cooperation and the role of the adult. Autonomy was encouraged in that the children selected and used the materials and resources of their own choice to pursue their own agendas. Many children had a clear goal or agenda, e.g. making cards and gifts for brothers and sisters.

Here is an example of a child selecting what she needed to make, what she had chosen to make:

> Zayba made a pendant with a piece of memo paper and raffia, using the hole punch. She then wrote on it lots of letter-like symbols. She explained that it was for her sister, Ifrah.

Here is an example of a child working on one particular schema: enclosure and enveloping:

> Aneesa made a border round the edge of her piece of card (with felt pen) and then coloured right into the middle. (She had been making borders in other contexts.) Next she made a border of stickers on top of this and subsequently filled the area inside completely with stickers.

Here is an example of a child using technology and invention to follow her interest in an everyday event – rain.

> On the main art activity table the children had been presented with egg-shaped coloured paper on which they were invited to stick milk bottle tops to make an 'Easter egg'. The adult concerned had left the room and Lianne had just duti-

fully made an 'Easter egg'. She took one of the egg-shaped papers over to the DIY table, and punched four holes in it. Next she cut some wool and asked me if I could make a knot. 'I'm making a raining hat' (it had been raining that lunch time). When her creation has been completed she asked me to try it on. I did so trying my best to hook the loops under my chin, 'Those bits are supposed to hook under your ears', she retorted, since I had been putting it on the wrong way. The other adult came back and Lianne showed her the creation and was complimented on having made a lovely Easter bonnet … to which Lianne retorted, 'It's a raining hat!'

Here is an example of a child asking the adult for help in her attempt to make something she needed in her imaginative play. Her need had been sparked off by something made available in the nursery.

Evelyn found a cardboard ring and a thin bit of cardboard tube. She brought these to me explaining her aim 'to make a magnifying glass' but said she didn't know how to stick the bits together. I suggested stickers and supported her in her efforts. On completion, Evelyn went off with it and used it in her imaginative play. As it happened, real magnifying glasses had been out for the children to use.

Here is an example of a child being highly motivated and struggling over time to fulfil her own goal.

Ishbel had made a mobile with bits of scrap, e.g. wire paper fasteners, and said it needed to 'hang'. An adult constructed a line for it to be hung on. Ishbel made her mind up that each day she would make a new mobile to hang on the line. Her next construction was difficult to hook on the line but Ishbel took her construction and invented a hanging device. The next day's construction utilised a wire paper fastener which she had pre-fashioned for the purpose of hanging it.

Here is an example of a child with special needs using the opportunities available to express his feelings.

Johnny was feeling frustrated – problems between him and his younger brother who was a newcomer to the nursery. Since his brother was involved with an

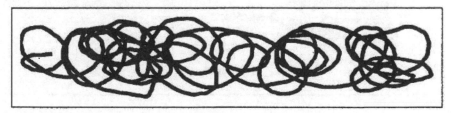

Figure 26.1 Johnny's coils of frustration

adult at the main activity table, he took himself off to the DIY table, where he picked up a piece of card and used felt pens to make whirling marks, seemingly displacing his anger and frustration (Figure 26.1) as his gaze was directed at his brother and adult. We know that he rarely chooses to do graphic activities.

Here is an example of a child finding resources and tools which allowed her to make something complex and intricate.

Olivia made a flower and the use of the cardboard tube at its centre allowed her to make it seem that the flower actually grew (Figure 26.2).

Examples of this kind of technology are clearly in contrast to what Prentice (1994) calls the narrow, skills-based approach to technology, associated with prescribed outcomes commonly in practice in many primary schools.

Here is an example to illustrate the role of the adult in supporting and extending learning. The adult acts as a physical scaffold as well as a cognitive one.

Edgar said 'I'd like to make a card for … 'I showed him where he could find all the paper and card, etc. [Edgar being a newcomer]. 'I want a folding and open-ing paper'. The day before, one of the adults had used pre-folded paper to do folding 'butterfly' pictures. Making this link I understood and showed him how to make such paper.

Matthews (1988) tells us that sometimes assistance from the adults is important, although adults should still observe and record important observations and show, by looking and listening, real attention to what the child is doing.

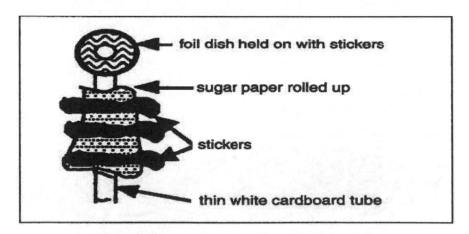

Figure 26.2 Olivia's telescopic flower

References

Jameson, K. (1974) *Pre-School and Infant Art*, London: Studio Vista.

Matthews, J. (1988) 'The young child's early representation and drawing', in G.M. Blenkin and A.V. Kelly (eds) *Early Childhood Education: A Developmental Curriculum*, London: PCP.

Prentice, R. (1994) 'Experiential learning in play and art', in J. Moyles (ed.) *The Excellence of Play*, Maidenhead: Open University Press.

Further reading

Athey, C. (1990) *Extending Thought in Young Children: A Parent–Teacher Partnership*, London: PCP.

Bennett, N., Desforges, C., Cockburn, A. and Wilkinson, B. (1984) *The Quality of Pupil Learning Experiences*, Mahwah, NJ: Lawrence Erlbaum.

Blenkin, G. M. and Whitehead, M. (1988) 'Creating a context for development', in G.M. Blenkin, and A.V. Kelly (eds) *Early Childhood Education: A Developmental Curriculum*, London: PCP

Bruce, T. (1987) *Early Childhood Education*, London: Hodder and Stoughton.

Bruce, T. (1991) *Time to Play in Early Childhood Education*, London: Hodder and Stoughton.

Bruner, J. S. (1980) *Under Five in Britain (Oxford Pre-School Research Project)*, Oxford: Grant McIntyre.

Hurst, V. (1991) *Planning for Early Learning: Education in the First Five Years*, London: PCP.

Lally, M. (1991) *The Nursery Teacher in Action*, London: PCP.

Moyles, J. (ed.) (1989) *Just Playing? The Role and Status of Play in Early Childhood Education*, Maidenhead: Open University Press.

Moyles, J. (1994) *The Excellence of Play*, Maidenhead: Open University Press.

Nutbrown, C. (1994) *Threads of Thinking: Young Children Learning and the Role of Early Education*, London: PCP.

Pile, N. F. (1973) *Art Experiences for Young Children*, Threshold Early Learning Library, Vol. 5, London: Macmillan.

Chapter 27

Transformation through music

The impact of classical music on the lives of township children

Rosemary Nalden

The last chapter in this part is one specially commissioned from **Rosemary Nalden** and it charts the remarkable work she is doing with young learners in South Africa. Look out for what she says about peer teaching, about the role of feelings in learning and about how she uses the discipline essential for being able to make music with other people as a teaching tool.

I first visited Soweto in April 1992, a month after a group of friends and I had organised a fundraising event involving large numbers of professional musician colleagues and friends who performed – or 'busked' – in some of the UK's mainline British railway stations to help a group of struggling township musicians.

Although I had followed the news and watched a few documentaries about South Africa, nothing had really prepared me for the surprises and shocks which awaited me. The string project for which we had been raising money was based in the 'washroom' (in other words, the lavatory) adjoining the stage of a rundown community hall in Diepkloof, a suburb of the vast sprawling township of Soweto. Next to the hall was a squatter camp housing several thousand people of African origin. It was a vibrant and exhilarating place, but also volatile and sometimes dangerous: inevitably a source of fascination for a middleclass, middle-aged white Englishwoman.

However, what probably took me most by surprise was the single-minded determination to learn classical stringed instruments which I encountered amongst the children attending the project. They bombarded me with requests for lessons, and then stayed all day in the stuffy little washroom to observe their friends' lessons. At this stage I was merely a fascinated onlooker giving a bit of advice to an established project, but I could not resist suggesting that, with such levels of motivation, perhaps it made more sense to involve *all* the children, including those who were watching, in some sort of group activity. Group lessons, albeit on a fairly basic level, were thus introduced to Soweto. Ultimately, these groups would change not only the learning habits of these youngsters, but, through the constant interaction with their fellow musicians during weekends and school holidays, their social habits as well.

Over the next few years I visited Diepkloof once or twice a year, with growing interest in and affection for the young musicians whom I was gradually getting to know. On a few occasions, we organised week-long Christmas camps in the bush where we combined intensive group instrumental study with outdoor activities and environmental awareness sessions. Around 40 children from the Diepkloof Project would attend these courses, at which I began to introduce various new techniques. (The group teaching approach was derived from what I had learnt from my close association with Sheila Nelson when I started teaching privately in London in the early 1970s, and subsequently during a brief exposure to the Tower Hamlets 'whole class' string teaching project which Sheila led.)

Through my increasing contact with these youngsters, I was able to address some of the problems which I felt were inhibiting their progress. Given their unique learning circumstances – often little family support, very few frames of reference, the constant need for self-motivation – it seemed to me that my first job was to 'empower' them with the ability to read music with some degree of fluency, which would give them a modicum of independence. Most of them had been taught in the old Suzuki-style – learning to play a piece by ear *before* reading it. But their teacher, offering random help with no specific system, had given them only the most basic music-reading skills. To go backwards, in other words to require that they now learn to read the music *while* hearing it, was a painful process, especially for such musically gifted children. I vividly recall marking out the five lines of a giant stave of music on the floor of the Diepkloof Hall and getting the youngsters to 'walk' the notes; thereby teaching them the basic concepts of reading from left to right, and of the way in which, like pitch, the notes go up and down the musical stave – concepts which musicians take for granted but which some of them found really hard to grasp.

Now – as we have done for the past decade – we introduce some rudimentary music-reading to all our beginners *from the very first lesson* to avoid such imbalances; the methods we use are far more sophisticated, thanks to the informed research of the *Stringwise* team which produced the series of teaching manuals *The Essential String Method Books 1 to 4* (1999) which we now use as a matter of course for all our beginner classes. In giving all our students the skills they need to be able to read music fluently to professional level we have also helped to dispel the myth that people in townships cannot read music. (This misconception dates back to the period when historically disadvantaged black choirs learned music from sol-fa charts, rather than from notation.)

With my insistence that these youngsters learn to read the music they were playing, different problems began to emerge. Soon I identified a common reason for the slow progress of a few of the children, which still crops up on a regular basis. Many township children have undiagnosed eyesight problems – possibly caused by the proximity of dust-filled mine dumps. When these are addressed, these children show marked improvements not only in their playing but also in their schoolwork and general self-confidence.

Furthermore, the emphasis I was placing on music-reading inevitably had a negative effect on body usage. Concentrating on a page of tiny hieroglyphics, then translating that information into physical movements which produce sounds, most of them pretty basic, very easily gives rise to the wrong sort of physical tension. Eagerness to 'get it right' can result in tightness, which in turn causes the scratchy sounds familiar to many parents whose children have just started learning a stringed instrument.

In any case, I had already observed some degree of stiffness in many of the students, which I felt did not tally with their ease of movement in other activities. At the bush camps in particular I saw that these African youngsters approached all their outdoor activities with such flexibility and lack of physical inhibition that I knew it should be relatively easy to introduce movement and flow into their playing. The key lay in teaching them the sensation of free flowing movements through tapping into their natural mobility. This was achieved by using a judicious choice of repertoire (at that time, a combination of Sheila Nelson's music, and the teaching repertoire commissioned for the Paul Rolland/University of Illinois String Research project) as well as group sessions *without music*, where they played rhythmic patterns on the four 'open' strings of their instruments. This had an immediate liberating effect – the violin, viola and cello became organic extensions of their bodies rather than impediments to flowing movement. (Many years later we were fortunate to acquire the services of a qualified Alexander teacher, Nanette Andersen, whose lessons in our music school, by placing the emphasis on generally healthy usage, greatly complemented our teaching approach.)

Group playing of these patterns focusing on freedom of movement is now such a fundamental part of our teaching process, even at quite advanced levels, that without it I doubt we could have achieved the remarkable fluidity in performance which characterises the Buskaid Ensemble.

Many people have remarked on the fact that, as Africans are naturally rhythmic, this sort of exercise must come easily to these children. Yet on the few occasions that we have accepted a child from another project we find that we have to work hard to *teach* that child to blend rhythmically into the group. The temptation to impose a regimented external pulse on the group should in my opinion be resisted; rather, the children should be encouraged to acquire visual and aural awareness of one another and build a sense of 'corporate pulse', which after all is what will make them into fine musicians in all their ensemble activities later on.

Vital as it was to give these children confidence in reading, there was another predictable side-effect. Focusing on what they *saw* rather than what they *heard* meant that their already somewhat dubious intonation[1] slipped even further. For many of them, singing was something you did in church; few township schools had school choirs. With the introduction of singing (using solfa) into the group lessons, they began to play far better in tune. The Ensemble's frequently faultless intonation is remarked upon far and wide and can be attributed to a combination of the youngsters' ability to hear what they read and their keen musical ears. We have had quite a number of children who have started off at Buskaid believing that they cannot sing – many of them boys, whose voices grumble and groan in low registers. Without exception, all have learned to pitch accurately and enjoy the added pleasure of singing together.

By 1997, increasingly concerned about the way in which the original project was being mismanaged, I had made the momentous decision to open a new music school in Diepkloof. Despite the fact that I found myself exposed to all kinds of new and sometimes unpleasant challenges, I was now able to develop some of the ideas which had until then been more experimental, given the constraints of my infrequent visits and the fact that fundamentally, I was helping someone else's project. Now my new 'music school', which was also in Diepkloof, consisted of a tiny shabby room next to the priest's office in a Lutheran church. Two dogs, permanently chained up in the yard outside, barked and howled continually, which I found extremely upsetting. Teaching aids were a small collection of music and an overhead projector. All practice took place outside. I often wonder whether, had we started off with sophisticated premises and fancy equipment, the results would have been any better, and have concluded that, despite all the discomforts, they would not have been very different. Passion to teach and learn music – mine, and that of my 15 or so pupils – was the driving force which kept us all positive and motivated in very adverse conditions.

However, because of the insistent and incessant demand for lessons from the local community, within a year I was already searching Diepkloof for larger premises. In May 1999 we moved into our own purpose-built Music School. By this time I had, with difficulty, found a few Johannesburg-based teachers prepared to drive into Soweto, which meant we could increase our intake of new students. When my assistant violin teacher, whom I had trained and given responsibility for the new beginners group, left suddenly, I faced a real emergency. As with almost every seemingly insoluble problem that arises in Buskaid, the solution had entirely positive consequences.

In this community I had already seen how older children took responsibility for younger siblings, relatives and friends. Boys and girls alike show great affection for small children, with no signs of self-consciousness in physically demonstrating their feelings. In our little musical community there seemed to be a natural tendency for more advanced students to help new learners. Why not channel this instinct to help into something more formal by introducing some teacher-training, and appointing 'official' assistant teachers from within the group? It would certainly obviate the need to rely on outside help which, with a few exceptions – our Alexander teacher, our cello and bass teacher, Sonja Bass and our piano accompanist, Jill Richards – has sadly not been dependable. Moreover I had also noticed that, despite their inexperience as teachers and their lack of formal training in the approach we were using, there was a kind of osmosis in our students' interaction with the younger pupils, which sometimes produced better results than all our sophisticated teaching methods! Thus began our highly successful teacher-training programme which has continued unabated ever since.

Nearly all our group sessions take place over weekends. During a typical class, each of the three or four assistant teachers in the room will be asked to take over an aspect of the lesson – singing a new piece to solfa, teaching a new rhythmic pattern using a system of time names, teaching a known or new aspect of technique, or leading a simple improvisation set. One of the most important and difficult skills to acquire is 'hands-on' handling of the pupils. Demonstrating a free flowing bow arm will help some children to imitate successfully what they observe, but most need to be physically assisted. The teacher herself must approach the learner with complete freedom and know exactly how to move the body and left or right arm in a manner which allows the pupil to get exactly the right physical feeling. I will often ask one of my assistants to guide my bow-arm in order to assess whether he is using unnecessary pressure, or perhaps not *enough* firmness in his 'hands-on' teaching. The detail is all-important. For example, one of our teachers is very tall and needs to be reminded that he has to come down to the level of his smallest student to avoid inadvertently lifting the child's arm or instrument higher than its natural level. In all these aspects of teaching, feedback from all of us will be immediate and sometimes vociferous!

Something which struck me very forcibly when I first started working in Soweto all those years ago was the way in which a whole class of children remained mute when asked the simplest of questions, a situation I found enormously frustrating. The explanation I was given was that in many township schools in those days, children were taught very much by rote and punished if they gave wrong answers. (I was told that physical punishment was rife in most of these schools.) Since a lot of my teaching revolves around problem-solving and lateral thinking, I was greatly challenged by this very narrow approach to learning. However much I reassured the children that it was fine to risk a wrong answer, it still took a very long time to shift their thinking. Many years later, the first generation of students I taught are themselves very frustrated and indeed puzzled by the same lack of response in some of the children they are now teaching. When I remind them gently that they reacted in exactly the same way, they find it impossible to believe!

In the first few years of learning to play a stringed instrument there are many fine skills which need to be mastered and which require patience, discipline and control. Holding both the instrument and bow in a way which is both comfortable and balanced, making an attractive sound, playing the notes accurately, rhythmically, and in tune: all require a great deal of detailed work on the part of teacher and student. During this time, apart from being taught to read music, the child will have been introduced to a number of concepts, including those of pitch, pulse and rhythm, bow speed and bow division; the ability to hear whether a note is sharp (too high) or flat (too low) and to effect an accurate correction – and many more besides.

One of my favourite challenges to even the most elementary group is to get the children to 'multi-task'. For example we may teach them a simple round which, to begin with, they sing in groups. Then we may number each child randomly so that they are now standing next to someone singing a different part. Finally, we may ask them to play an 'open string' accompaniment as they sing. From my observation of their responses, I wonder whether many of them are ever similarly challenged at school!

Very early on we introduce them to the delights of playing in ensembles. Sheila Nelson has written a number of pieces with variations, for upwards of 14 parts, where every level from very beginner to advanced is involved. Now their early rhythmic training will stand them in good stead if chaos is not to ensue.

In the next stage of their development a tempting carrot is offered. Since all the students are learning in the same building, they regularly hear other groups and individuals playing, practising and rehearsing The ultimate goal for every student is to play in the top ensemble. To this end some, but not all, will put in hours of extra practice in the hope of joining an ensemble they know is famous and performs regularly both in South Africa and internationally.

But here, new and more sophisticated demands are made on them. They will have been taught different types of bowing and left hand techniques to suit different styles of repertoire, but now they may be required to apply their knowledge and make a musically appropriate choice whilst playing far more challenging repertoire. They will also be acquiring a far more sophisticated grasp of phrasing in music, which they have learnt is similar to punctuation in a piece of writing and the rise and fall of the voice in speech. Many of them, however, will now be expressing their own unique musicality which will far transcend the skills and techniques they have been taught. Among our students, who after all come from a tiny area of a vast township and have been accepted on a random basis, there is an exceptionally high percentage of these musically gifted and responsive children.

I am often asked – by musicians in particular – how it is that our students seem to possess such an uncanny sense of musical style. I suppose the word 'educate' in its true meaning is still the best way of describing my process of teaching style and interpretation to these young African musicians, because I feel that most of them are already endowed with a deep, instinctive knowledge of what the music is saying and how to express it. My craft is to tap into and develop those gifts. This is why their music-making has such integrity: because they feel so much from very deeply within. For me, making this discovery about them from a very early stage was a source of great excitement and is part of the miracle of teaching at Buskaid!

Initially, however, there had to be a simple means of putting the music into its historical context. When I first came out to South Africa, it took me quite a long time to digest the fact that I was teaching youngsters with absolutely no knowledge of European traditions or culture. I still get caught out, even now, when an Italian term, whose linguistic derivation is completely obvious to me, doesn't spark any glint of recognition in my students. I can remember teaching them their first reel, and asking them what they knew about Scotland. One brave soul volunteered that it was somewhere in Italy. Actually this made my teaching far more creative, and the process of describing – as graphically as possible – the historical context of a piece of music, whether it is a Viennese waltz, a Bach concerto or the Elgar Serenade, has provided me, and I believe, my students, with much enjoyment over the years. There isn't a single Buskaid student (including the smallest beginner) who doesn't know how to waltz! And before I am accused of 'cultural imperialism', being able to waltz constitutes no threat whatsoever to the fundamental African-ness of these youngsters: that's far more likely to occur when they turn on their television sets.

Other disciplines, which will have an impact on the rest of their lives, will be imposed, some of which they may find unpalatable. My reputation for being extremely strict stems I believe in large part from my unflinching insistence that every child should arrive on time for every rehearsal. 'African time', a phrase with which I am horribly familiar, simply means that it's OK to be late. But we are constantly at pains to point out that an orchestra is also a metaphor for any engaged community. Its success, both in its organisation and in performance, depends entirely on the committed participation of every single member.

For a whole decade until the end of 2007, some students dedicated every Saturday and Sunday afternoon, excluding school exam periods, but including school holidays, to orchestral rehearsals. Many of them also spent up to 16 school holidays touring abroad (which, while a great privilege, was also extremely hard work), often returning to school the day after a long international flight. Not only did this tough demand on their leisure time keep them 'off the streets' but it also provided some of them with a safe environment and family-like community they lacked at home. The day the mother of two young students died quite unexpectedly, they both arrived at the Music School in utter shock. We were performing that evening, and to my amazement they still wanted to come. Playing music surrounded by their friends was the greatest source of strength they knew.

One of the many rewards I have enjoyed as a result of my teaching of these young African musicians is to observe their remarkable progress. Kabelo was brought to Buskaid from another project – unusually by his mother – when he was 11 years old. He had spent the best part of a year learning very little and being extremely bored. For a couple of years he continued to associate the violin with the negative experience he had had at the other project and I despaired of getting him motivated. At around the same time, a highly active and exceptionally talented 10-year-old, Simiso, arrived on our doorstep, also from another project, also unstimulated and very frustrated. The combination of Kabelo's lacklustre presence and Simiso's frequent noisy interruptions in the same class tested my patience to the limit. At the end of 2001 we took the whole group out into the bush and were intrigued to observe the two boys spending hours together under the trees playing endless duos. By the end of the camp, Kabelo was hooked. He is now, together with Simiso, our most advanced student and the current leader of the Ensemble. I recently observed him performing and saw in him a violinist of such natural effortless talent, so completely at one with both the music and his instrument that I knew that all the work, both his and mine, which had gone into creating this young artist was utterly worthwhile. The sheer *physical* pleasure he takes in using his instrument to create deeply-felt beautiful sounds and musical phrases is a joy to watch. In him I see the fulfilment of my aim as a teacher to create a violinist whose technique and musicality are, literally, in total harmony.

At the other end of the spectrum, we have Kgotso, who arrived at Buskaid with his older sister. He was 4, she was 8 – and his babysitter. To keep him occupied I gave him our smallest violin, a one-sixteenth. Five years later he is one of the most promising children we have ever taught. As with very many of our students,

Kgotso lacks the presence of a father; in his individual lessons he is taught by my most senior assistant, Lesego, whose contact with him on a one-to-one basis is not just about teaching him the violin; Lesego, a grounded and mature young man, is a perfect male role model for Kgotso, giving him added stability in his life as well as helping him to fulfil his passion – to become a great violinist!

I vividly recall the first time I saw Mzwandile. We were busy rehearsing one Saturday afternoon when a very small boy sidled into the room. He was quaintly dressed and wore very large spectacles. I assumed he was someone's little brother until an elderly lady came forward to introduce herself. She was, she explained, his adoptive parent. Abused and then abandoned by his natural mother while still a baby, he was fortunate that she had happened to see his story highlighted on local TV. Three years later she had also seen Buskaid on television and decided that this was the perfect project for her small charge, despite the fact that she had to travel across Soweto by public transport to reach the school. I have never established quite how she found us, but she now brings him three times a week, twice for groups and once for an individual lesson. To begin with Mzwandile was an added difficulty in our already overloaded lives. At the age of three, he could not read and, damaged by the horrific start to his life, was quite disruptive. I suspected, however, that he was far more aware of what was going on in the classes he was attending than he made out, a fact backed up by his Granny who reported a lot of violin-playing activity at home – far more than we could elicit from him in the school. Now at the age of eight he is showing signs of real musical talent and often inadvertently demonstrates some skill he has obviously worked on at home but is still trying to keep a secret.

In a society that is male-dominated but female-led, in other words where women are still considered inferior in many ways to men – but very often assume greater responsibility, particularly in childcare – girls can grow up with little confidence in their abilities and talents. A decade ago, the project had far fewer girls than boys and those girls were shy of taking a leading role in the ensemble. Now the statistics have changed dramatically – girls outnumber boys, and several of them are prominent as both teachers and performers. Keabetswe (18 years old) is in many ways typical of the changing face of female society in the townships. Her mother brought her to Buskaid nine years ago; she was a timid and rather sickly child. A few years ago her mother remarried and moved out of Diepkloof, leaving Keabetswe in the care of her grandmother and an aunt. Challenged by this change in her circumstances, Keabetswe showed remarkable courage and maturity. In the past couple of years she has assumed a far more responsible role in the ensemble, holding her own in the first violin section, which consists mainly of boys. She is also one of Buskaid's senior violin teachers, a job she does with flair and confidence.

Two founder-member violinists with two very different stories are now both professional musicians. One, Samson, whom I heard for the first time at our 1994 bush workshop when he was a 10-year-old beginner, is now freelancing with a number of major British orchestras, having gained a Bachelor of Music with First Class Honours from one of the UK's leading colleges of music. Samson grew up in a shack opposite the Diepkloof squatter camp and, until he was 13, slept on the floor of the shack with his younger sister. Recognising in him a highly motivated and gifted violinist with great potential, we decided to pay for his secondary education at an Arts School in Johannesburg, subsequently funding his study at a music college in England. The other, Gift,[1] who had no contact with his father and whose mother was a domestic servant, was also highly talented but older than Samson; he had already got himself into a few scrapes, and around the time Samson left for the UK, Gift left Buskaid. For five years he battled a major drug problem, and virtually stopped playing. Living alone in a shack with no outside support, somehow Gift realised just before it was too late that he did have a future because of his solid training as a violinist. Against all odds he managed his own drug rehabilitation and in 2008 returned to Buskaid. With a great deal of support from his fellow students and his teachers, he is now playing with the local professional symphony orchestra. For me, both young men are extraordinary for their achievements against all odds; but perhaps Gift's journey is more remarkable: as a typical township youth of his generation, beset by all manner of temptations and problems, he is a wonderful example of a soul saved by music.

A question I am often asked and hard put to answer is – why the violin? A decade on from the founding of the Buskaid project we still get many children pitching up to the music school, often without a family member, with the request to learn the violin. When asked why, the answer is always the same; 'Because I like it and I like that sort of music'. Historically, there seem to have been generations of violinists, often related, who have somehow managed to access teaching, even in the difficult days of apartheid. Yehudi Menuhin's visit to South Africa in the 1950s was certainly a source of inspiration to one black violinist whose subsequent activities ultimately spawned a number of township projects. But it still intrigues me that on the whole, the desire to play a stringed instrument seems to come from deep within the child who somehow or other senses that he has a special talent which must be nurtured.

While the impact on any child exposed to classical music – and more especially to the discipline of learning an instrument – is universally recognised as being entirely positive and beneficial, there are undoubtedly benefits unique to the Buskaid project, given its location, its place in the history of the country and the particular community it serves. In the past ten years much has changed in the 'new' South Africa and there are now more opportunities for children growing up in the townships. But some conditions still prevail: unemployment, overcrowding, crime, drugs and HIV/AIDS are challenges faced by millions of young Africans. There is no doubt that the Buskaid project has profoundly influenced the lives of every single one of its students in countless different, positive, life-affirming ways.

Note

1 On January 11, 2009, Gift's mother found his body on the floor of his shack. He had been killed and his body dragged back to the shack. Despite all our efforts to find out what happened there is still no information forthcoming from the police.

Rosemary's remarkable and moving account provides a link to the last part of this book – a new venture looking at what happens when adults start to learn something new for the first time. Each of the contributors refers back to prior learning and its effects on learning something new and you may well try and analyse what is similar and what is different between the 'early' learning of young children and of adults.

Part VII

Learning
A second chance

In this, the last part of the book, we change the focus completely. We move away from the learning of young children to look at the learning of adults who decide, sometimes later in life, to learn something completely new to them. Each of these adults share the frustrations of developing a new and complex set of skills – in much the same way that a young child learns to cut or ride a bike or climb a tree or use a skipping rope. Each adult brings previous experience to the task – in some cases experience that is helpful and in some, experience that causes dissonance. As you read the small case studies of adults learning something totally new for the first time in their lives, look out both for the threads they have in common with early learners and the differences between the two groups:

- The ways in which academic study of things like grammar and syntax can provide a structure to understand a new 'language'.
- The role played by social expectations on learning.
- The importance of peers and the group on learners.
- The joy of sharing with peers, without language being essential to the exchange.

The contributors to this section are three viola learners, Gillian Gould, Richard Gartner and Sandra Smidt, and one sculptor, Jenny Thornley.

Chapter 28

Late early learning

A 64-year-old begins to play the viola

Gillian Gould

Nothing in an exclusively verbal academic life had prepared me for the joys and difficulties of starting out on learning a musical instrument. Choosing a string instrument meant immediately that the physical skills involved were far less daunting than learning to swim in this wholly new wonderful sound world of timbre, rhythm, melody, harmony and counterpoint. The safety net of a fixed pitch instrument like the piano wasn't there: where in the ether did these elusive notes lurk, to be reliably summoned without anything to which one might relate their pitch? And this fairly heavy, cumbersome thing didn't even support itself on legs or a stout metal spike, yet both one's hands are needed to be constantly in motion! So in all its formidable terrors this felt very like that first day at school, when initiation into impenetrable mysteries awaits.

Yet, of course, in some ways it was very different. At my age, the social anxieties and fear of making a fool of oneself are no longer a deterrent. My memories of my early days at school are dominated by social anxieties, both in relation to peers and what seemed frequently capricious adults. I feel as though anything I learned then was incidental to negotiating these minefields! Learning as an adult in the supportive environment of other adult learners and positive mentors is a great deal easier. And a whole lifetime of experiences makes for a less bumpy ride: the daily business of dealing with the world is less traumatic and beset with significances than it was for a little child. Only in the fact that throughout that lifetime listening to music had been an important source of pleasure and emotional endorsement did I encounter an unexpected irony: what I might have hoped would be a help was a depressing deterrent when I began to make noises that fell so far short of what I knew to be the potential of the music and the instrument. I realised that when my children learnt musical instruments in their early childhood, no expectations, no memories of definitive performances complicated their joy in the discovery of music and the acquisition of this new skill. I haven't found a way of countering these inhibitions, born of knowing what this music can sound like and the length of time required to learn enough to do it justice – an unachievable aim at my age, when it is clear, too, that physical and mental agility are diminished.

But the other side of this increased awareness brings huge satisfactions. My years of studying literature and its central place in my intellectual and emotional life give me access to the structures and syntax of this new medium of music. And its essentially ephemeral nature has a poignancy for the old which the young can, I almost hope, only faintly sense. It is wonderfully liberating to move in a non-verbal language, which can express everything that words can, without their contingent limitations.

There are pleasures accruing to the business of learning and playing when one is old which I hope one shares with the young. People who get together to make music gloriously defy categorisation by age, social class, colour or creed and the relationships formed between folk who, in other contexts, would be improbable companions or who would never have had the opportunity to meet, are a delight. The deterrent of not sharing a common spoken language is immaterial: a powerful factor in the practice of all the non-verbal arts. It is a truly transcendental experience to lose oneself in the creation of something bigger than the sum of its parts, in being subsumed in a coherent organism which is committing everything to the temporal suspension of self in the realisation of the composer's intention. It involves a sort of empathy, with the other members of the group, with the composer, with the audience, that I would like to feel was common to all musicians, young and old, great and aspiring!

Chapter 29

A second string?

Sandra Smidt

I was 61 years old when I first decided to learn to play the viola. In a beginners group at the East London Late Starters String Orchestra (ELLSO) I met Gillian Gould (whose piece you may have already read), along with other people, younger and older – all of us beginning the frightening and complex task of learning to play a stringed instrument and all of us coming from very different backgrounds and experiences.

From childhood I had played the piano and classical music was always central to my life. I grew up in a home where music was played all the time on the gramophone and my parents took me to classical concerts, such as they were in South Africa during the apartheid years. I was in the school choir and in my early adulthood a friend taught me to play the flute as payment for having her lovely son live with us during the school week. When I retired I joined a chamber music class, playing the piano in a variety of string groups and I found that very unsatisfactory. It seemed to me that the piano dominated and I envied the string players the intimacy of their playing when they played without the piano.

I bought a cheap scholar's viola set and looked online to find a teacher. The young woman I selected was cheerful and jolly and treated me as though I were the age of her young school pupils. She chivvied me along, gave me smiley faces when I played a simple tune and absolutely refused to let me try and speed ahead, which was what I badly wanted to do. Our partnership lasted only a brief time when I went off and joined that remarkable organisation, the East London Late Starters String Orchestra. Every Saturday morning I had the opportunity of group tuition in technique, simple ensemble playing and musicianship. Compared to some of the other people who started when I did I was at an advantage. I could read music, knew the values of notes, understood key signatures and could count. But I was also at a disadvantage. My previous experience was both a plus and a minus.

Having spent my life as an educator I was fascinated by the teachers I encountered. Many of them had had no formal training as teachers and were natural and instinctive teachers – respectful of our efforts and interested in our progress. Some were astounding in terms of how carefully they prepared for each session and in how well they matched the tasks and the music to our needs. Some dealt with us learners who were generally much older than they were with humour and tact. And some managed to understand that as older adults we were in a hurry: perfection at each stage was not something we felt we had the time to strive for.

Learning to play the piano had required me to learn to read both the treble and the bass clef. I have no memory of how I learned that just as I have no memory of how I learned to read. People around me did it, expected me to do it and I did. But now, with the viola, I had to learn a third clef, the alto clef. And I found it incredibly difficult. I could easily enough learn which finger to put on which string, but to this day – nearly 3 years on – I still struggle to name the notes. It seems to me that my previous experience and knowledge creates some cognitive dissonance which my fellow learner violists are not necessarily experiencing. I also find it incredibly difficult when a piece of viola music has a section in the treble clef. I see the treble clef on the page and panic. Given time I can work it out but cannot just read the music by sight. Like a small child asked to decode a text without clues or context, the fear and panic immobilise me, destroy my confidence and cause me to fail.

Playing the piano means having to read two clefs at the same time. Playing the viola only requires reading one line of music: in a sense this is easier and sight reading does not cause me enormous difficulties – except when there appear to be many small notes on a page. So here my previous experience seems to help me.

What first fascinated me about playing the viola was the requirement of having to actually find or make each note. On the piano or the flute the notes are there – defined, existing, and largely inflexible. On the viola a light shift of the finger changes the tuning and the tone and allows for enormous flexibility and the possibility of creating fine shadings in tone. Tuning is something I still struggle with although now playing with a range of friends in string quartets is beginning to train my ear.

Most help of all in playing music is my experience of having listened to a great deal of music throughout my life. Now that I have reached the dizzy heights of being able to play with friends in string quartets I find that my knowledge of the music puts me at a real advantage because I know what the music I am playing should sound like. On the other hand I also know that what I sound like is quite unsatisfactory when compared with the remembered music in my head. But it is a remarkable and entirely satisfying journey I have embarked on and something I could not have done without all those features of early learning which apply, equally, to what Gillian Gould calls 'late early learning':

- To succeed I need to be involved in what I am learning and to enjoy it, even when the challenges sometimes feel overwhelming.
- To succeed I need peers around me to share the journey, some of whom act as models, some as teachers and some as learners.
- To succeed I need teachers who communicate their love of music, know what and when to praise, know how and when to intervene and and support and recognise the particular learning needs of older people (for example worsening eyesight).
- To succeed I need to be offered music to play which is 'real' music just as young learners need to learn through real and meaningful activities.

Chapter 30

Musicology to music-making

A late learner becomes a late starter

Richard Gartner

I am a member of the East London Late Starters' Orchestra (ELLSO) where, like my co-authors Gillian Gould and Sandra Smidt, I am a violist who has learnt the instrument from scratch with this ensemble. The viola is, in fact, the first instrument I have played in my life, having had no opportunities to do so at school and having assumed, like so many others, that it would not be possible to learn one later in life. I am in the perhaps unusual position of beginning practical musicianship with a degree in music already in my possession; the year before joining ELLSO I had completed a degree from the Open University in this very subject.

The Open University is one of the few institutions where a subject such as music can be studied with no prior experience, practical or academic. I started taking a level 2 course, *Understanding music: Elements, techniques and styles*, which teaches music from scratch, and assumes no knowledge of music or even an ability to read it. With the practical skills (such as harmonisation) and the solid theoretical background this course provided, I progressed to more advanced ones in which I learnt musical analysis, major trends in music theory such as gender studies and reception theory, and music editing skills.

In all of this, my only exposure to the practical business of music-making was the summer school of the first course, where theory became practice to a small extent. Music-making sessions were part of the timetable and those such as myself with no experience or instrument were gently pointed to a choir and asked to participate vocally. For the first time, I found myself following a conductor's beat and joining others in the collective experience of producing music. It was a number of years after this that I found myself holding a viola at my first ELLSO session.

To have studied music academically is certainly to be given a theoretical background to how music 'works', which can be of great help when starting to learn an instrument: not for nothing is theory part of the standard grade exams that school children so well know and love. At the most basic level, a knowledge of how to read music is going to be essential to playing in an orchestra, although even this is not necessary at the ELLSO which will teach the new learner how to do so. Slightly more advanced knowledge, such as understanding how keys work (a complete mystery to me before I took my first Open University course) undoubtedly makes life easier for the novice music-maker. All of this is well under one's belt after any academic study of music.

To study music does, of course, allow one to gain a broad knowledge of repertoire in a variety of genres. This always helps with interpreting music as a musician by giving the performer greater insights into what composers are trying to do in their works, how they are typical of their period or genre, and what features to expect in a piece. Such knowledge can, of course, be acquired by the keen listener without academic study, but there is nothing like the requirements of a course curriculum for making sure this is achieved.

In some specific areas, the academic study of music can give the performer perspectives which are not necessarily easy to acquire otherwise. A sense of musical structure, for instance, which is so vital to classical music, can help the player become more of an interpreter, and academic study can really assist here. This is true even in the relatively short pieces that beginners at the ELLSO begin to play. For a more advanced musician, a knowledge of how, for example, sonata form works is going to be very important as so much of a work's emotional message is tied up in its structure and the relations between its components. Again, it is not necessary to go so far as to take an entire degree to gain this appreciation, but it is one way to do so.

Beyond the broad musical structures that academic study may allow the musician to appreciate, an understanding of lower-level features such as harmony and texture may also give insights into what part a given instrument should play in the overall musical scheme of a piece. Viola players often fill in the harmony of a piece and a knowledge of how harmony works can make it easier to appreciate the role of their parts and make the process more than just churning out the notes. Similarly, knowing something of orchestral textures can be very important for violas which often occupy the middle of the aural landscape: knowing, for instance, the difference between a contrapuntal or homophonic texture can be important for knowing how prominent a given part should be, which ones should carry the main weight of the musical argument, and how one should articulate one's own. Much of this can be acquired by experience, of course, but an academic background certainly helps.

All of the above certainly suggests that an academic background can help novice performers find their way to interpretative literacy, but there is the occasional drawback to taking this route. After studying music academically, sometimes to quite an advanced level, one finds one becomes an infant again when picking up an instrument for the first time. Knowing how music works can make the sometimes painfully slow rate of progress as a learner somewhat frustrating, as practice lags behind what one knows in one's mind is possible and desirable. This is likely to be a problem for all adult learners, not just those with an academic background in music; we are inevitably more self-critical than children starting to learn, and so more liable to frustration.

Perhaps a greater problem that is specific to those who have studied music academically is an almost inevitable temptation to treat music-making as an academic exercise rather than an emotional one. Knowing something of how music works in the abstract may lead one to be overly analytic, seeing music-making as a problem to be solved rather than a form of emotional expression. It is perhaps one of the most remarkable features of music that a seemingly abstract concept, such as a sequence of chords, can carry such an emotional charge: thinking too much about how features such as this are constructed can certainly detract from feeling their emotional impact. The tendency of academic study to dissect is not necessarily the best training for the synthesis that is a musical performance. This can certainly inhibit one becoming a musician rather than a mere translator of music from its notated to its aural form.

Studying music academically does from my experience give a valuable background of theory and repertoire that are very helpful to the novice musician, making the whole learning curve somewhat less steep. But it is still steep enough, and frustrations may arise if one expects the theoretical to smooth one's way to the practical more than is reasonably possible. Although every orchestral musician does require some degree of background knowledge to be able to function effectively, this does not need anything as formalised as degree-level academic study to acquire: if it did, the number of musicians would be far smaller than it is today. The theoretical may help form the background to making music, but it is the foreground that counts, and this is where the bulk of the effort in becoming an instrumental player needs to be directed.

Chapter 31

Becoming a sculptor

Jenny Thornley

The first 4 years were bliss. I threw myself into making sculptures of bits of women's bodies, working every hour I could find outside my work hours and often in the night. I was 55 and had never been taught how to paint, draw or make sculptures. I felt free. There were no rules and I was doing it for myself.

I began by painting a picture of my teenage sons. Both had struggled through school with communication difficulties and life had been hard. I wanted to express complex feelings about them and thought I might try writing a book. But it was impossible to find the words to describe my experience. I'd wanted to be an artist since I was five but had abandoned art at school when I was 14 because I thought my dad said art wasn't a serious subject. He wanted me to do physics. So that's what I did and I hated it. When I had painted my picture I cut it up and reassembled it. Soon afterwards I attended a music summer school which included a small art module. I painted another picture. It was bold and suggestive of three dimensions. The art tutor encouraged me to make a sculpture. It was so exciting to create something using my whole body. With trepidation, I bent myself creakily around a piece of wood and chicken wire and forced my muscles into action. The best bit was putting my arms around the finished piece.

By the time I got home, I knew I'd carry on making sculptures. That's what I've done for 7 years. My subject matter has been about feeling old. I am 62. I make sculptures of what it's like to feel ugly and invisible. Friends tell me how young I look but they are old too. We all crave the same flattery. The truth is that I now draw my pension. My body is decaying. It's soft and wrinkled. Bulges have appeared around my middle. I worry about what's going on inside. At my age it is impossible not to think about death. That gives a sense of urgency to what I do. It makes me get up in the morning and focus.

But the state of my body is only one aspect of ageing. There are so many good things. My mind is alive. I can still run for a bus and play cricket on the sand. I can drink wine and laugh at silly jokes. And I know who I am now. Well, not quite. Best of all, I don't have to conform to a stereotyped image that the media would like to force upon me. My house soon filled up with torsos, slashed tubes and bulging ripples of rubber.

Then I blundered into art college to do an MA in Fine Art. I sent an envelope of photos of my work and was invited for an interview. I had no art qualifications at all.

I'd been a town planner, a researcher in local economic development, an adviser to workers' cooperatives, a gardener, and a dyslexia teacher and finally I had become a speech and language therapist. I was offered a place at art college. The course involved choosing a project to work on. There was no teaching. We saw our tutors regularly and discussed progress. From the first day, everything about the place puzzled me. I had two degrees and a diploma. I'd done 10 years of research. Yet there I was, struggling to understand what I should do. I didn't seem able to transfer my past experiences into this creative environment. The other students were all much younger and seemed to know the rules of the game. Most had been through the art system, whatever that was. They were speaking a different language. I felt lonely and was beset by fears of failure and of being an imposter. Each criticism from my tutor felt like a major blow. I had to summon all my inner resources to keep going.

My friends were crucially important. They understood what I was trying to say in my art. Some even bought a sculpture. I went back to my music summer school and had an exhibition of my work there. Soon after that I took part in an Open Studios weekend; lots of locals came through my front door and gazed at my strange creations. I was desperate to know whether I was communicating or not. It seemed that I was, sometimes. That gave me the confidence to carry on with the difficult process of learning my new trade.

The problem was not the sculptures themselves. I had plenty of ideas. I could make my body parts out of plaster, paper mâché, foam tubes or whatever I could find. It was challenging but straight forward. The problem was to understand the creative process, to have the words for it. There wasn't much time. When I was a child I wasn't even aware of a learning process. It just happened. In slow motion. I did what teachers required of me. I developed from a rote learner into an analytical thinker. Neither was it like the degree I'd taken 10 years earlier in speech and language therapy because that was familiar territory. I stuffed my brain with information, used it to analyse real people's speech problems and chose therapies to help them. This was a creative field and felt very different.

But the learning process seemed to be a closely guarded secret. More likely, the tutors just didn't know what I didn't know. Gradually, I discovered how to develop a creative idea. I worked really hard. I read too many books and made too many sculptures that led nowhere. I watched what the other students did and asked questions. Often I asked the same ones, over and over again to different people, tutors, art students, friends, anyone. Suddenly someone would say something that made sense and I'd leap forward another few steps. Eventually I learnt that the creative process was about taking a single idea and following it through a process of experimentation, describing what happened to the materials, to the visual images produced, the feelings it produced. I learnt how to push materials to their limits, take risks, and learn from failure.

Afterwards it all seemed so straight forward, so obvious. Why couldn't someone have demystified it all for me at the beginning? Maybe I could have achieved so much more. But that's unimportant. I got through it.

Now I have lost some of the freedom or naïveté with which I attacked my materials so joyously when I first started. But the learning I did has made me more self critical and reflective and I understand what I'm doing better than anything I've done in the past because this time I had to find the words for what it was all about. It's still a thrill to walk into my art room.

A last word

The search for the 'crock of gold'

Sandra Smidt

At the end of the first edition of this book, there was 'a last word' – a philosophical statement about the underpinning philosophy of the book which was that the early years of life are crucial and that what is learned during those years influences learning and attitudes to learning throughout life. I hope you find evidence in this new edition that this is still true. All of those who have contributed to the book share this view and all seek to describe their thoughts on how children's learning can best be recognised, analysed, enhanced and respected. But I hope that in this edition there is evidence of a move away from holding only models of development rooted in industrialised Western societies to seeing development more broadly and recognising the value of diversity in family structures, ways of child-rearing, views of childhood and the roles of others. At the end of the first edition, I quoted Martin Woodhead, who, in his booklet *In Search of the Rainbow* (published by the van Leer Foundation in 1996) discussed how important it is to remember that there is more than one way of viewing childhood and child-rearing. He argued that quality can only be defined when the views of the community – their values and beliefs – are taken into account and respected. When searching for 'universals' in discussing quality he urged that care be taken.

I hope that more care has been taken in this edition and that the 'universals' still emerge in the chapters in this book. They include the following:

- Children learn through following their own interests and concerns as they seek to make sense of their world. We might say that the same is true of adults.
- Children learn in a social and historical context, primarily through interactions with others.
- Learning involves the use of cultural tools developed within cultures over time and these include language, music, art, dance, technology, material tools and symbolic systems.
- Those working with young children should be respectful of what they are paying attention to: only by doing this can they really engage with the children in a way which will enhance learning.
- Seeing children as competent from birth allows those of us involved with them

to give them opportunities to share their competence with their peers. Children cannot only learn but teach.

- Children learn through many things. They learn through play where they are able to follow their own interest. They learn through watching more experienced others. They learn in situations where the purpose is evident to them, where they can have direct experience and where they can build on their prior experience.
- They learn when they feel respected, valued as individuals, cared for as people with feelings. They learn from the experience, ideas, views and feelings of others, through stories and music and theatre and dance and so on. Learning is multi-faceted and complex.

The strength of the first edition was the diversity of the voices in it. I have tried to keep this diversity and offer my thanks both to those who contributed to this edition and to those who offered pieces which we were not able to include because we needed to keep the number of pages down in order for the published book to be affordable. The first edition ended with a quotation from Woodhead, which is repeated here:

When I was in Kenya during my fourth round of visits, I was beginning to wonder whether the word 'quality' had any substantive meaning at all. As we drove back to Nairobi, the sky was filled with a magnificent rainbow. This experience suggested a perfect metaphor to encapsulate the search for quality. English children are told the ancient Celtic legend, that if you dig at the rainbow's end, you will find a crock of gold. I later learned that African children learn a similar legend. It seems to me that trying to pin down 'quality' is a bit like trying to find the crock of gold at the end of the rainbow. We may make progress in the right direction, but we never quite get there! Children learn that the rainbow's beauty is real enough, but the 'crock of gold' exists only as a cultural myth. In the same way, I want to argue that those involved in early childhood development must recognise that many of their most cherished beliefs about what is best for children are cultural constructions. As with the rainbow, we may be able to identify invariant ingredients in the spectrum of early childhood quality, but the spectrum itself is not fixed, but emerges from a combination of particular circumstances, viewed from particular perspectives.

(*In Search of the Rainbow* 1996: 9)

Index